strategy execution made easy

D1740956

drivers

a story of transformational change

Glenn Price & Terry Reynolds

Grosvenor House
Publishing Limited

This book is published by
Grosvenor House Publishing Ltd
28-30 High Street, Guildford, Surrey, GU1 3EL.
www.grosvenorhousepublishing.co.uk

The characters and events in this story are fictitious and any resemblance
to reality is merely a happy coincidence.

A CIP record for this book
is available from the British Library

ISBN 978-1-78148-485-2

With Foreword by
Dr. Joseph Folkman,
Co-author of the best-selling books
*"The Inspiring Leader: Unlocking the Secrets of How
Extraordinary Leaders Motivate"*,
*"The Extraordinary Leader:
Turning Good Managers into Great Leaders"* and
'How to be Exceptional'.
www.zengerfolkman.com

Illustrations by
David Lewis
www.davidlewiscartoons.com

Acknowledgements

You might skip past the acknowledgement in a book, ready to dig into the good stuff. But we believe that there are a few words worthy of your attention before the story even begins.

We would like to express our gratitude to the many people who encouraged us to complete this book; to all those who provided support, talked things over, read, wrote, offered comments, allowed us to use their remarks and assisted in the editing, proofreading and design.

Of special note, we wanted to highlight the early development of the Vision to Results model by Jim Robertson. The model has certainly been further refined and tested, but it wouldn't even exist without Jim's original curiosity.

We would also like to take the opportunity to thank the many clients around the world who have been part of our research, strengthened the model, and reaped the benefits of embedding the Vision to Results framework in their organizations. It couldn't have happened without you—the leaders.

Foreword

Dr. Joseph Folkman

I grew up in a small town in the Western United States, in the state of Utah, called Logan. To make extra money and to keep me out of trouble, my mother got me a job working for my Uncle Chester who lived in a smaller town called Providence. My uncle was a farmer. I vividly remember a clear spring day when my uncle asked me to jump in the truck and he drove to a field on the outskirts of town where he grew wheat. At the end of the field I spotted his yellow Caterpillar tractor parked and hooked up to a plow. My uncle turned to me and announced, "You're going to plow!" I was 12 years old, I had driven his other tractor once or twice before but the Caterpillar looked bigger and more powerful. All I could think of was, "Cool, this is going to be fun!"

My uncle was an excellent teacher. He sat down in the tractor seat while I stood behind him and looked over his shoulder. He explained how to start the Caterpillar tractor because the process was a bit different with a diesel. He showed me how to turn the tractor because it did not have a steering wheel, rather two levers that controlled each track, and he taught me the basics of how to plow. He then plowed up the field, turned around and plowed back down. When we got back to where we started he stopped the tractor and announced, "Now it's your turn." I got in the seat and right before I was ready to move forward my uncle said, "The most important thing about plowing is to plow straight and stay about two inches from the furrow on the left track. I confidently announced, "No problem" and started moving forward. In order to stay two inches away from the furrow I leaned over to the left side of the tractor and watched the track, constantly adjusting the distance between the furrow and the track. When I got to the end of the field my uncle said, "Now, look back and see how you have been doing." What I saw was a wavy furrow not a straight line. My efforts to try and keep the tractor two inches from the furrow caused me to constantly adjust the tractor to the right and then back to the left. After I turned and stopped the tractor, my Uncle Chester said, "I am going to teach you a principle about how to plow straight." He said, "Look down at the end of the field. Do you see that fence post straight in front of us?" I looked down the field and saw the post. He then said, "Aim for the fence post!"

It turns out that when you "Aim for the fence post" you can plow straight. My experience on the tractor is very similar to the experience many employees have in organizations. They are trying to do a good job. They want to deliver results. They know how to do their job well. They have been given very specific instructions but they are looking down. They make lots of adjustments but they are still looking down. They are focused on the specifics of doing their job well but they are not focused on the vision. When people are confused about the vision or they are not focused on the vision, the result always suffers.

In my consulting work with organizations, I have told this story hundreds of times along with data, models and processes. At the end of a speech or a workshop I often ask people what they remember. They can sometimes recall that I presented some data. They might know where a model is located in their workbook or where they can refer to a process, but for some strange reason they can repeat the specific details of this story almost word for word. Glenn Price and Terry Reynolds could have given you hundreds of pages full of data, evidence, models and processes; instead, they have provided a compelling story of an organization going through profound change. They include a summary of principles and process at the end of each chapter— but what you will remember when you are in a similar situation, is not the models or the process steps, it is the story. By remembering the story you will recognize how you can move forward and what you can do. I contend that the story Glenn and Terry tell is not fiction; it is a story they have seen repeated hundreds of times in different organizations, it is very consistent and predictable. Read the book. Remember the story. Reflect on the principles. You will find they provide you with a fence post at the end of your field.

Content

Part One

Set Direction

Chapter One

Vision

Scott Boylan measured his client's moods as much with his ears as his eyes. Even so, the client didn't need to say a word. Scott just needed the first five seconds after they opened the car door. "They're giving themselves away from the moment they grab the handle," he told his younger drivers. "By the time they've sat down and put on their seat belts, I know whether they're happy about where they've been, or glad to be going where they're going."

Then again, you didn't always need a decade's experience to read a mood. This morning's first passenger snatched at the door and sank into the seat as if he'd like to shut out the world for good. Those moods, Scott knew, called for less, not more.

"Straight to the office, Mr. Dalton?"

"Just drive, Scott," said the man in the tailored suit, pushing a hand through rain-wet hair. "Anywhere except the office."

Infinity Investments was Scott's biggest account. He and three of his five drivers spent most of their time driving the staff of Infinity from home to the office, from the office to meetings, and home again, but often via a dinner or function. He knew where they all lived, where they went on vacation, and when they went on vacation because it was Scott or one of his drivers who took them to the airport. A father of young children himself, Scott knew which children played tennis and which ones loved to ski. To the children, Scott was a happy sight in his dark suit and black tie. His arrival meant the beginning of vacation adventures. To his clients, he was sometimes the first face they saw on a bad day. Today was obviously one of those days for Alex Dalton.

Scott checked the road over his shoulder and slid the town car away from the curb and into the drizzle. If the CEO of Infinity Investments wanted to put off going into the office with a circuit of the city, Scott wasn't going to ask questions.

In the back, the CEO followed the raindrops on the window as the motion of the car pushed the water in random patterns. Scott glanced at him in the rearview mirror. The CEO was a trim man who was quick to show interest in the world and the people around him. When you added up all the journeys over the years, the two men had talked for hours. They'd discussed the news of the day, the economy, and their children. They'd forged a particular bond over their frustrations with the sports teams they had continued to support, despite the let downs and heartbreak each man's team had brought him over the years. Today, however, the CEO's shoulders were high and the usual light was missing from his eyes.

The red lights of the cars in front dragged tracks in the wet road as Scott kept a steady pace in the inside lane. Five minutes passed before the CEO broke the silence.

"I'm sorry, Scott," he said, meeting the driver's eyes in the mirror. "It's been a hell of a week. A hell of a month, actually, but that's no excuse."

"That's all right, Mr. Dalton. You know I'm happy to drive you wherever you want to go, or nowhere at all, even on a morning like this one."

"It's just nice to be moving, frankly," the CEO said, turning back to look through misted window.

"It's been a tough few years for all businesses, Mr. Dalton," said Scott, guessing his passenger wasn't talking about the traffic.

"You know that feeling when your car isn't going anywhere but the cars next to you are?" the man in the back said, meeting Scott's eyes in the mirror.

"When you feel like you're going backwards?"

"Exactly. You feel like you're moving, but you're just standing still. And standing still in business is dangerous. If you're standing still and your competitors are going forward, you might as well be going backward."

"It sounds like a difficult time."

"I'm sorry again, Scott. I don't mean to be as miserable as this weather or to talk in riddles. But you read the papers... like you say, it's a tough market. I've been there before, but now everything seems to change every 10 minutes. I've got managers telling me all the time their teams are asking where we're going and what we're going to do. At the same time, I've got the board on my back demanding results. I'm not sure they read the papers. It's always the same. Numbers. Quarterly targets. Half-yearly targets. I don't know where they think these numbers are going to come from. Should we go this way? Should we go that way? It's nothing but guesswork. Half my competitors are going one way and the rest are going the other."

"Infinity's a big company, Mr. Dalton," said Scott. "Surely it's not just you? You must have some help making these calls?"

"My team seems to have more opinions than there are people. Everyone's looking for answers, and I don't have anything more than questions myself. Some days, it feels like it's taking everything I've got just to stop us actually going backward instead of just feeling like we are. If standing still is taking all my energy, I don't know where I'm going to find the energy to get us somewhere else."

"Have I ever told you how I choose a new driver, Mr. Dalton?"

Alex raised an eyebrow and turned away from the blurry shapes through the window. "I don't think you have," he said.

"The interview's probably not what you'd expect," said Scott. "It's certainly not what they are expecting."

Scott had left the army a sergeant. After 20 years' service, he'd kept the haircut and upright bearing but had decided he wouldn't be taking orders anymore. Looking for a business that wouldn't keep him locked in an office, he had bought a car and applied for the right permits. With hard work—something else he'd taken from the army—and a commitment to service, his business had grown to three cars and five drivers working in shifts. Scott was a natural leader and his drivers liked working for him so driver turnover was low. When he did have to hire a new driver, he was meticulous in the selection.

"I have to be careful," he said to his passenger. "My business is in their hands every time they pick someone up. I can't be there when they're on a job. If they don't give our clients the sort of service I want to be known for, they could lose me that client for good, and I might not even know why. People often prefer to say nothing when they don't like something and they just find another company. So I'm looking for more than a clean driving record and the right number of years of experience. I'm hiring a person, not a checklist of qualifications or milestones."

"A literal collection of milestones in your case," said Alex, smiling for the first time that morning.

"That's right," said Scott, catching his client's change of mood in his mirror, "and those milestones are passed in the driver's seat. But I'm giving the person I hire responsibility for growing my business. I need them to sell the experience because clients who enjoy travelling with us tell their colleagues and friends. That's how the business has grown and that's why my drivers all start in the back seat."

Scott explained that after going through the formalities in his office, he'd take the potential new driver outside to the firm's newest town car and tell them it was time to go for a drive. Invariably, the driver would start for the driver's door before they noticed

Scott holding open the rear door for them. "Where to?" he'd ask.

"The thing is, Mr. Dalton, there's more to driving than just driving." He paused for a moment while he concentrated on merging with a line of slow-moving traffic. "You can tell a great deal about a person from where they want to go. Sure, it takes some coaxing. They're drivers; they're used to doing the asking. But once they realize that I'm serious, they give it some thought. They have to. It's not a metaphor: we can't go anywhere until they've picked a destination, and that tells me a lot about them."

"What can you tell about someone from that?" asked Alex, shifting to a more upright position in his seat.

"Some of them want to drive around the sights or head for the upmarket parts of town, seeing it all from the back seat of a smart car for a change. They tend to be the ambitious ones. Others want to drive past their kids' schools or their mum's house. They're the ones who work to give their families everything they need. We're all doing the same job but we're not doing it for the same reasons."

While Scott chauffeured a potential driver, he told Alex, he would explain to them his business philosophy.

"The speech is always the same. I tell them driving's our business, but getting the client from A to B is only the start. If you want repeat business, you need to pay attention not just to the way you're driving but the route you're going to take to get them there. Sometimes it's easy, but sometimes you get the best result from a less obvious route. The drivers who get and keep the sort of clients I'm aiming for are the ones who know driving is just the start." Scott had found an open stretch of road and the car was moving again. "But who am I telling, Mr. Dalton? You've been with me since it was just me driving. There are thousands of drivers for hire in this city. Obviously, they all know how to drive, and for the most part they all know how to get from A to B. If my business were just about being able to drive a car around the city, it would be no different from a hundred other companies, maybe a thousand. My business grew because I knew being successful in this game wasn't going to be about being a better driver; it was going to be about giving clients a better journey."

In the back seat, Alex had his chin in his right hand and was nodding in agreement. A light had come into his eyes.

"People talk about their drivers all the time," the driver continued. "Mostly, they talk about them to complain—too chatty, too opinionated, and too heavy on the brakes. I wanted to build a company people talked about because we got everything just right. We're there on time; we've already thought about the fastest route; and we'll let you know if we're expecting any problems on the way. We talk, if the client would like to chat, and we keep quiet when it looks like they want time to think. And people do talk about us. Almost all my business comes from people recommending us and it's not our driving they're talking about, it's the journey."

Scott heard the rustle of the CEO's suit on the leather upholstery as Alex shifted in the backseat.

"Scott, you're a wise man," said Alex, leaning forward to touch him on the shoulder. "I'm ready to go to the office now, but if you'll excuse me, I've got a call to make on the way."

Alex pulled his phone from his pocket. "Kirsty," he said to his assistant on the other end, "I want the leadership team in the conference room as soon as they come in."

It seemed to Heather Wong that the boss almost bounced into the conference room. Heather had begun her career in her native Hong Kong, where she had honed her skills reading body language because so much was often left unspoken. She was seldom wrong, especially about Alex, whose open management style was one of the things she most liked about him. As Alex crossed the room, there was more length in his stride than she'd seen for a long time. She chose to take it as a good sign. In other jobs, unexpected calls to meeting rooms first thing in the morning hadn't signaled good things, especially for the head of HR. Infinity Investments had been sailing through some choppy waters, but this morning the captain of the ship didn't seem too worried. He seemed—could she be right—excited?

Alex caught the eye of each of his team as he walked the length of the conference table. Heather was the first person he saw. She sat in her usual seat—nearest the door, with her back to the conference room's impressive view of the city, a tall waxed paper cup of coffee on the wide boardroom table in front of her. Heather was respected by all for her ability to balance the needs of the business with the needs of the individuals who worked for it. Her counsel was often sought and was always available for the price of a coffee.

Next to her was Kathryn Chivers, a Hermes scarf adding a splash of color to her conservative suit. The communications director was the oldest of the group. Her reputation was for sharp insight and discretion.

Michael Stockley, Infinity's sales director, sat a few seats apart. A bull-necked man with close cropped hair, Michael had started on the trading floor back when greed was good and worked his way to the executive level on the back of exceptional numbers and dogged determination. He looked up from his iPhone to catch Alex's eye as he passed. The newest member of the team, his undiminished enthusiasm for meeting his sales targets led to the occasional tense conversations with anyone he felt was getting in the sales team's way.

The team rippled forward almost imperceptibly as Alex passed. He knew he had their attention. The only member of the team not to move was Lee Washington, the CIO. He was visiting one of Infinity's offshore data facilities, so hadn't been able to make the impromptu meeting in person. Instead, he was represented by a three-legged Polycom unit. Because no one had spoken, he didn't know the CEO had arrived or seen for himself the glint in his boss's eye.

Arriving at the whiteboard, Alex turned his back to the room and began to write. He could sense those in the room craning their necks behind him, straining for the first inkling of what the impromptu meeting was about. He heard Michael put his phone down on the table. When Alex turned around, there were three questions behind him on the board: Who are we? Why are we here? What do we believe?'

Alex looked down the table, smiled, and spread his hands expectantly. For a moment, all they could hear was the sound of the rain tapping on the windows. Alex looked at each of them, saying nothing. No one spoke.

"Lee, are you there?" Alex asked the speakerphone on the table.

"Yes, Alex," the CIO replied.

"Okay, I've just written three questions on the board. Answering them is the sole agenda item for this meeting. They're: Who are we? Why are we here? And, what do we believe? Anyone?"

"Well, my name's Michael," said the sales director eventually. "I'm here to make money, and I believe I should be out there now making some calls to do it."

The joke fell flat, although he had earned the silent appreciation of his colleagues for being the first to speak.

"That's good, Michael," said Alex, "but, I mean it. They're important questions. Without answers, we can't really know what we're trying to achieve. We've never set aside time to ask them and, if we answered them for ourselves, we've never talked about it as a group. I've made a mistake in not making sure we set aside some time to think about these things as a team. What is this business for? What is our purpose? And why are we the right ones to be pursuing it, if indeed we are?"

"Do you mean, 'If indeed we are pursuing that purpose'? Or are you saying we are pursuing it, but we might not be the right people?" asked Kathryn, a red teardrop earring swinging like a pendulum as she tilted her head, looking again at the three questions on the board.

At the other end of the line, Lee stopped absent-mindedly replying to emails and started paying closer attention to the meeting.

"Either. Both," said Alex. "And, if we are the right ones to be doing it, what do we need to change to do it right? At the same time, if someone told us we had to make changes, what would we say we were definitely keeping because it was truly working? What is it that we believe in as a group that has got us this far and that might get us further?"

"I find these sort of existential questions are generally best left to HR," said Kathryn swiveling her chair to face Heather, an arch twinkle in her eyes.

"Sure. Push the big questions to HR. We can handle it," said Heather, turning away from Kathryn. She unclenched her jaw as she said to Alex, "Maybe you need to help us out a bit, Alex. It's still early and I'd have ordered a bigger coffee if I knew I'd be tackling the meaning of life today." She took a sip of her coffee, looking expectantly over the rim at the CEO.

"Fair enough, Heather," said Alex, pulling out the chair at the head of the table and sitting down. "The questions are big, but not quite that big. If we get on to

the meaning of life, I'll get Kirsty to order you an extra big coffee. For now, I'm talking about us, Infinity. It was a nice swerve by Kathryn, but maybe she's right. You're at least in the best position to answer the 'who' questions. You know more about our people than anyone. If we look at the company, what sort of team have we built? Do you think it's the right sort? Are we all like Michael—here mainly for the money? Or is there something else that brings us to work?"

"Not to state the obvious and, loath as I am to agree with Michael under most circumstances, the pay is good and Infinity has a pedigree," said Heather. "There is a money element, and we're not a bad name to have on a resume."

"We're in financial services. Of course it's about the money," said Michael, his neck flushing red. "We're a good name to have on your resume when you go for another job, one that's offering more money. If you're in this business of all businesses and it doesn't come back to money for you, you're in the wrong place."

"Sure, but we don't pay more than anyone else and there are plenty of good names out there," said Alex. "Do people just end up here because it's where the chips fell? Or, as Michael says, because it's a rung on the ladder to the next place?"

There was a silence in the room.

"I know why I came, if that helps," said Kathryn, breaking the tension. "You know where I was before and you know their reputation. When you work there, work is what you do. It was like Eisner said at Disney, 'If you don't come in on Saturday, don't bother coming in on Sunday.' Work was all you'd do because you didn't have time for anything else. I heard Infinity was different, and I wanted to try it."

"And what did you find?" asked Alex.

"I found I stayed," said Kathryn. "I liked it. I still like it. It amazed me that the quality of the work was just as good and so were the results. I wish I'd come sooner."

There were nods around the table and a "me, too" from Lee on the speakerphone.

"That's also true for a lot of our people," said Heather, acknowledging the nods. "They've done the other thing. They thought working 70- or 80-hour weeks was the way to get ahead. If you left before midnight and weren't back again before 7 a.m., you weren't serious. That kind of thing. They come here when they want to see if there really can be more to life than work, without giving up doing what they love to do."

"Infinity. Where tree huggers look after your investments," said Michael, "but only until 5 pm. No wonder we're in trouble." He reached for his phone again.

"You don't need to be a tree hugger to want to have more to life than an inbox that never empties, no matter how much time you spend on it," said Kathryn, pointing at the phone in Michael's hand. "Believe it or not, there are people who think it's possible to do a great job and still have horizons wider than a couple of 27-inch monitors, the bar across the road, and a home they never see in the daylight."

"What's wrong with the bar across the road?" said Michael, looking genuinely puzzled. "It's the best beer in the city."

"I think that's right," said Heather, ignoring him and looking from Kathryn to Alex. "We don't put it in the job ads, but people ask me about it when they come for an interview. They've heard we're not the same."

"And you, Michael?" said Alex. "Seriously, is that why you're here? For the money and the adjacency to a decent microbrewery?"

"Are you asking me if there's more to life than selling investments, Alex? Because you know there isn't. Not for me."

"Come on, Michael," said Lee laughing down the telephone line. "We know you're a master of the universe, but even you aren't the Wolf of Wall Street."

Outside the drizzle had stopped and the sun had begun to burn through the clouds.

"All right, you got me. I did come here because I'd had enough. I love my work, but there's more to me than that. One day, I'll show you my watercolors, Kathryn," he added, to general laughter. He put his phone back on the polished wood and slid it away from him. "You all know I've got a family and of course I know I've got a family, but I didn't properly realize that for a long time, if I'm being honest. I missed a few too many school plays before I got the message. I do love what I do, but after a while I wanted to see if it was possible to have more. I would not have said this before, but that's why I called when I heard you were looking for a new sales director."

"Thank you, Michael," said Alex.

"Now that I've gushed," said Michael, "Alex, what do you mean 'What's our purpose'? I don't want to come over all Jordan Belfort again, but it's not complicated, is it? We're here to sell investments to anyone who'll buy them."

"Family man status aside, you're not what you'd call a layered person, are you Michael?" said Kathryn, putting her head to one side and looking at him quizzically.

"I was reminded, on the way to work this morning, that it's a mistake to take a business at face value. What we do has to be more than just selling investments," said Alex. "Hotels don't just sell rooms with beds in them. They sell experiences. You choose one hotel over another for a number of reasons, but part of it is the experience you'll get and part of it is knowing what that hotel values. This one is about exceptional service. That one is about comfort or efficiency or convenience or expense or whatever. Boiling it down the way you are, Michael, there's nothing to choose between one hotel and another. At their most basic, they're all collections of rooms with beds. On that basis, in our business, we're all just firms with investment products. You'd only ever choose one on price."

"You're right," said Lee, who was at that moment actually in a hotel he'd chosen because it always remembered his preferences, regardless of where he was in the world. "If you said 'Hyatt' to me or 'Hilton,'" The Plaza' or 'The Savoy', I'd instantly have an image in my mind. I have an idea what they stand for, and why I'd choose one and not the other."

"Assuming you had the money to make a choice," said Michael.

"Yes, Michael, money is part of it," said Kathryn. "No one is disagreeing with you about that. But Alex is right. We've let ourselves become indistinguishable from everyone else. We've forgotten why we're in this business and who we're in it for. And if we're the same as everyone else, then there's no point in our being here."

"And if we can't see any point in our being here ourselves, why on earth would a client choose us?" added Heather.

"Look, I do take your point. I'm not a complete idiot. I just think sometimes you forget what makes every-thing else possible around here," said Michael, a blade of annoyance coming into his voice. "If we think we're attracting people to work here because we're so different, why don't we offer clients the same thing we offer our own people?"

"What do you mean?" asked Alex.

"Offer them a life-changing investment."

"You mean only offer them high-risk investments?" asked Kathryn.

"No, not high-risk, not necessarily," said Michael. "A big return would change some people's lives, but so would a big loss. An investment that brought financial peace-of-mind would change some people's lives. For others, it would be knowing they could put a child through university. What changes one person's life might be different from what changes another's."

"So, the thing would be getting to know why the customer is investing, and putting them into investments that could really get them there," said Kathryn, furrowing her brow and nodding slowly. "I like it."

"Infinity. Life-changing investments. It works," said Alex.

"It works for clients, and it works for everyone on the team," said Heather. "We make an investment in the people who work here. We pay what the rest of the industry pays, but we trust people to do great work in a reasonable time. We don't treat them like we pay by the hour and we've bought all the hours in their day."

"I agree," said Lee's voice from the speaker. In his hotel room, he stood up walked over to the window. It was sunny outside, approaching lunchtime. On the street below, he could make out people bustling from one place to another. They looked so similar from up here, but every one of them represented a history, a family, and a collection of individual hopes. "If we think about this from the customer's point of view, it's exactly why they invest. They are looking for something more. Money is an end in itself for some people." Michael felt a few eyes turn to him. "But I'd say, for most people, it's a means to an end. There's something they want it for. We have a lot of data on our existing customers. We can start asking some really smart questions about what 'life changing' might look like for different groups."

"What I really like about it is that it's big," said Alex. "You can imagine people rallying to a vision like that, but it's still possible to see how you, as an individual employee, fit into making that happen. It's more than a slogan. It's definitely a destination you can aim for. So what would you say were the beliefs that've gotten us this far—even if we didn't realize those beliefs were what was holding us together?" said Alex.

"A belief in people," said Heather, leaning forward. "We believe that people don't need to be pushed to the limit to do a good job. In fact, they probably don't do a good job if they're always operating at their limit."

"Also, we believe we do it differently," said Kathryn. "We believe it is possible to stand out and be different in this industry; that we're not all the same."

"And we believe there's a value to that difference," chimed in Lee.

"I believe we've fitted a missing piece," said Alex, holding out a hand and chopping the air to punctuate his thoughts. "We know why we're here, we know why people want to work here, and we know why our customers are going to join us. Because we're not just about investments."

Around the table, his team leaned back in their chairs.

"It's been a good morning's work, and I would give you the rest of the day off, but we've got lives to change. And now that we know where Infinity's going, we need to talk about how we're going to get there. I'm not unrealistic. I know you've all got projects on and full schedules, so I'm not going to ask you to clear your diaries and stay here to talk about it today."

"That's a relief," said Michael. "I've got four client meetings today."

"Like I say, I'm not unrealistic," said Alex. "So, we'll say, tomorrow morning at the same time. I shall look forward to your ideas."

A shaft of sunlight came through the window behind Heather, catching her cup as she finished the last of her coffee.

Vision to Results Insights

They don't know it yet, but the leadership team at Infinity has stumbled onto the Vision to Results (VTR) framework for ensuring business success by sharpening leadership focus and aligning strategy, developing competence, and inspiring behavioral change. In reality, the framework has taken years to develop and it continues to evolve as we partner with clients—including many household names—to deliver amazing results from working through Vision to Results.

At the end of each chapter of Infinity Investment's story, we will be pulling out the VTR lessons from the story. You'll see that none of it is complicated; indeed, some of it seems blindingly obvious—when it's pointed out. It's entirely possible that a company might stumble onto VTR as a winning formula, but our experience has been that few companies have all the elements in place and even fewer have them all working smoothly at the same time, and certainly not by luck.

As the name of the model suggests, having a vision is especially important.

The importance of having a vision was one of several important reminders and insights Alex had in this chapter:

1. Your vision is your destination, so without a vision you're going nowhere.

2. A leader needs to set aside time to think about that vision and should think big: whether the vision is aspirational or conditional, a poverty of ambition will not inspire anyone.

3. The vision needs a concrete element or it just becomes a marketing tagline, not a destination people can be motivated to reach. Infinity is in a position to really change people's lives. Leaders and team members can use the vision as a compass or litmus test when deciding whether a decision or proposed action is a good idea for the organization. In contrast, you couldn't run all your choices through a marketing tag line like "Just Do It," even if it would simplify the decision making considerably.

4. The vision needs to authentically fit with the values of the organization because you need your people to want to achieve it, which they won't if it goes against what they believe in.

5. Finally and all importantly, the vision has to represent a destination for the organization that your customers are interested in and buy into, so leaders need to look at the vision through customers' eyes before deciding on it.

*   *   *

Chapter Two

Strategy

The weather was not the only thing that had brightened by the evening. It was a visibly happier Alex who slid into the back of Scott's car.

"Home, Mr. Dalton?"

"Yes, please, Scott. And thank you," said Alex, putting a finger over the knot of his tie and working it down.

"I haven't got you there yet, Mr. Dalton, but thanks in advance is always appreciated."

"Well then, thank you for that in advance, Scott, but what I really meant was to thank you for what for what you said this morning about knowing who we are and why we're doing what we're doing. It really got the ball rolling for us. For the first time in months, I know where we're going. Of course, all we have to decide next is what we specifically need to do and how we're going to get there, but that's tomorrow's problem. At least we're not going to be standing still anymore."

"In that case, do you mind if I ask you a question?" Scott asked, flicking on his indicator to pull the town car into the outside lane.

"The way I feel right now, Scott, you could ask me anything you like."

"Do you know where you are?"

"Right now I know exactly where I am: on my way home. And, if the children will allow it, quite possibly I'll treat myself to last night's game."

"If that's what you're going to watch, you might not be in such a good mood for long," said Scott.

"No spoilers please, Scott. I don't care how badly they messed it up last night. I'm in too good a mood. I shall have a drink to their very good health, whatever happened."

"I meant: Do you know where you are in terms of you saying you knew how you're going to get where you're going?"

"Ah, well, that's another question altogether. I can't go into too much detail, although you'll have heard your fair share of the inner workings of Infinity driving us from meeting to meeting. In fact, in some ways, you'll know more about the company than I do, or certainly different things, some of which you'd be far too discreet to tell me, I suppose?"

"That's true, Mr. Dalton. More than my job's worth to talk about what I hear coming from the back seat, as you well know."

"Anyway, you'll know things haven't been plain sailing. I know I've got good people. I was reminded of that not half an hour after you dropped me off. But sometimes, it seems like I've got a team full of good players who don't where the goalposts are. Or, more accurately, they've all got their own ideas of where the goalposts are, so everyone's kicking in different directions. Everyone's tired from running around hard, but there's not been a lot of scoring lately. The team is still all over the place, even on the occasions when we agree where the goalposts are. So, in answer to your question, where we are would depend on whom you asked."

"With respect, Mr. Dalton, it sounds like it might not matter where you put the goalposts then."

"What do you mean, Scott?"

"Well, it's one thing to agree on where you're going, and that sounds great, but it's pretty hard to get somewhere if you don't know where you're starting from. I'm not saying what I do is as complicated as what you do, but if there's one thing I know a lot about it's getting somewhere."

"No arguing with you there, Scott. You always know where you're going," agreed Alex.

"That's definitely the easy part for me. I don't need to decide where I'm going; that's the client's job. But they do expect me to work out how to get there, even when they have opinions about it—and you and I both know people always have opinions about driving routes.

Luckily for me, we've got GPS now. Like I told you this morning, I've still got to make decisions, though. The GPS will give me options and even add in traffic information. That all helps, as does a little local knowledge."

"It's all true, Scott, but unfortunately there's no GPS for business, whatever the *Economist* and the rest of the business press like to suggest. I wish there were."

"True enough, Mr. Dalton, but my point is that the GPS is helpless without two pieces of information. From what you're telling me, you've only got one. If there was such a thing as a GPS for business, you'd be typing in where you want to go and the GPS would be doing absolutely nothing for you."

"I think I'd want to return it in that case, Scott. I don't expect a magical business GPS would've been cheap."

"Probably not, Mr. Dalton, probably not, except this one isn't broken. It can't possibly tell you how to get to your destination if you can't tell it where you are right now. The starting point is the second piece of information it needs. We forget about that part because we get in the car, switch on the engine, and the GPS automatically starts asking itself where it is before we get around to telling it where we want to go. The GPS knows it needs that information before it does anything else, so it never forgets to ask. But if your team hasn't agreed until today on where it's trying to kick the ball, can you be sure they've all asked themselves where they are starting from?

"I'm beginning to think, Scott, that we've wasted a lot of car journeys talking about sport and the weather," said Alex, sitting back in the seat and folding his arms.

The following morning saw Alex's team gathered again in the boardroom. The thousand mirrored windows of surrounding office blocks reflected white clouds and blue sky back into the conference room. The senior executives were clustered at the end of the table nearest the whiteboard. Heather had her coffee— an especially large one, Alex noticed. Kathryn, not one for a disposable cup, had brought in a Japanese teapot and a single discreet bowl. They all had notebooks in front of them. Michael, the most visual thinker of the group, had a few pens in different colors. And even he, usually the most eager to get through any meeting and back to work, had brought a bottle of water.

Alex was uncapping a marker pen when the door opened again and Lee walked in, wheeling a small suitcase behind him.

"I cut short my trip," he said, looking at Alex as he took a seat next to Heather. "This is more important."

Alex nodded and turned back to the whiteboard. On the right-hand side, he wrote the words "Life-changing investments." On the left of the board, he drew a question mark. On the opposite side, he drew a large cross. He drew an arrow across the board—from the question mark to the cross.

"Yesterday," he said, "we agreed we were going to stand out from the crowd by not just being any investment house. We asked what brings us together and what our purpose is as a company. The answers to those questions told us we want to become the investment house that changes lives. Today, we need to think about how we're going to get there. But we can't do that until we've answered one more question."

He took off the jacket of his suit and arranged it over the back of his chair at the head of the table. Turning back to the board, he pointed the marker pen at the cross on the right-hand side of the board. "This is where we're going. X marks the spot," he said, writing the words 'life-changing investments' under the cross.

"The question," he continued, circling the question mark in red, "is: Where are we now? If we asked our clients or our own people about us, none of them would say we're changing their lives. Getting to that point is going to be a journey, but we can't even start making plans until we're clear where we're starting from."

"When it comes to our people," said Heather, "I don't agree that we're not there already." She furrowed her brow, looking first at Michael and then at Kathryn. "At least two of the people in this room came here precisely because we offered them something better. From an employment perspective, I'd say we are already offering what we want to offer and people know about it. Isn't that what we talked about yesterday?"

"That's not entirely true," said Kathryn. "I'd heard from friends that things at Infinity were different, which was why I looked into it. There was no point in leaving the last place if that weren't true, so I made a point of asking Alex about it in the first interview. But I'm not sure I would have been bold enough to ask questions like that earlier in my career."

"Kathryn's right," said Michael, "which feels strange and unusual to say." Kathryn curled her lip at him and shook her head. "I felt the same as she did and I wasn't afraid to ask up front either, but I'm not sure my sales guys would feel comfortable asking in an interview if this is a nine-to-five place. That's the sort of question that would knock you out of the running in most places."

"Michael, you'd knock someone out of the running here if they asked that question," said Kathryn.

"True, but it's still better than other places," said Michael. "I've worked in jobs where you'd tell an interviewer you didn't have kids at all, let alone say that not only did you have kids but you expected to be able to see them occasionally."

"That's what the wife's for?" said Heather, raising an eyebrow.

"I'm just saying," said Michael, throwing up his hands and falling silent.

"If we're setting ourselves up as different, I'd say we've got to back it up," Alex cut in. "Word of mouth is powerful, but unless something is locked into your contract, it's not a promise and you're taking a risk that things aren't that way at all. If being a better employer is something we're serious about offering, then we need to offer it explicitly. We need to make a commitment. Heather, we're part of the way there, but I want you to think about how we're going to make a promise to staff that working here will be life-changing."

"I'll talk to my team, and come up with some ideas for how we're going to build it into our employee value proposition. If it's going to be explicit, we need to have it in all the messages that potential employees might see, whether it's our LinkedIn page or in what our external recruiters are telling candidates when we start hiring again. One thing's for sure, we won't have any competitors making similar promises."

"I'd like to work with you on that," said Kathryn. "What we're communicating to potential new employees will need to sound the same as what we're saying to everyone else. It's somewhere Communications and HR should definitely be working together."

"But we need some substance to be working from," said Lee. Like Michael, Lee had worked his way to the executive team from the bottom, starting his career by coding banking software. Alex's reminder that you couldn't make plans to get somewhere unless you knew exactly where you were starting from was second nature to a computer programmer. "We can't just guess how people feel about working here. As Michael and Kathryn said, not everyone is going to have spoken honestly about what they think when they came on board and we wouldn't have recorded it even if they had."

"It's a good point, Lee," said Heather. "We need to get a sense of what we're doing well and what we could be doing better so we know what we can promise based on what we have already and what we need to work on."

"We could take a survey?" Kathryn suggested.

"There are some good tools out there," said Lee. "I'll have one of my guys talk to you about what's on offer and how we can help you analyze the results."

"If you three can work on that together, that would be perfect," said Alex. "Which leaves you, Michael. How do we go about letting our clients know we're in the business of changing lives?"

"I haven't talked to my team yet, but I thought about this hard last night," said Michael. "It's a new focus for us. It's not how we've thought about products and positioned them in the past. I realized we needed a radical rethink. We need to look at every product from the bottom up, to see if it fits. If it doesn't, we'll see whether it can be reworked to fit. I can see more than a dozen products we can retire straight away, and I've got a few ideas for new ones, including an idea for an ethical fund."

"Retiring products that don't fit the vision is a good idea," said Alex. "Change isn't only about what we're going to start doing differently. We do have to think about what we're going to stop doing as well. But when you say an ethical fund, what do you have in mind?"

"We want to change people's lives, so why not have a fund that doesn't invest in guns or any kind of weapons? Maybe one that doesn't give money to projects that displace people from their homes or whatever?" said Michael.

"That's all very noble," said Kathryn, "but it's not exactly original. Investors have plenty of choices when it comes to ethical investments."

"I know that," said Michael, snapping his head towards the head of communications. "I'd need to look at what our competitors are doing to make sure ours is different. There will be a way to make it stand out. Maybe we could focus on investing in companies that are developing products with the potential to improve lives. Maybe we could find a way for customers to vote on what we invest in."

"A Kickstarter for an ethical fund?" said Lee.

"Something like that," said Michael. "Or at least a facility to give up-votes to investment choices within a fund."

"You're right that it's not original, Kathryn," said Alex, "but I don't think that's what's really wrong with it. We have to be clear when we say 'life-changing' whose life it is that we're changing. What we agreed yesterday is that we're about life-changing investments for our clients and everyone who works here. That doesn't mean we can't have an ethical fund, and I'd like to think we're already pretty careful about not putting our clients' investments where they'll ruin anyone's life. But if we're going to rally Infinity around a vision, it has to be crystal clear. First and foremost, I want our clients to know it's in their lives where we'll make the biggest difference. That's the primary lens we should look through when making decisions. Then, I want the people who choose to work here to know that working here will change their lives. If we can be a positive force in anyone else's life, that's fantastic, but it's not the focus."

"Point taken," said Michael. "I'll sit down with the team and work up some of my ideas, and see what they can come up with too. For our part, we know we absolutely have to have a portfolio that fits the vision."

"There's someone else you should sit down with, though," said Alex.

"Who?" said Michael.

"Our clients. We need to make sure we've got products that match our vision, but that's no good if they don't meet the clients' needs as well."

"I can have my team look at the data," said Lee. "We know a lot about our customers and what they want already. Just off the top of my head we've got web analytics and call center records to start with. We've had lots of feedback already; we just haven't been looking at it thoroughly."

"I think we need to start getting this down," said Kathryn.

"What a surprise, the head of communications wants to write something down," said Michael. Heather laughed in spite of herself. She didn't usually like to encourage Michael when he baited other members of the team.

"Now, what could a salesman have against keeping things honest?" said Kathryn, and even Michael had to smile. "I'm not talking about anything over-engineered, just a plan on a page so we're clear on who's doing what."

"That's a great idea, Kathryn," said Alex. "Before we start, can I say what a breath of fresh air it is that we're all in agreement about this? We're not going to be able to do this if we're going off in different directions. Let's get down on paper what we're going to do after this meeting. Michael?"

"Top of my list is making sure our existing products fit the vision of life-changing investments. Next is coming up with some new funds, ones that really stand out. And making sure everything we offer meets client needs."

"What do you see being the most important things to do there?" asked Alex.

"For the existing products, it's a review. I'll divide the products among the team and ask them to hold each one up to the light. Does it have the potential to make life better for the person who invests in it? For the new products, my team needs to have a brainstorming session, and we need to check what we come up with against what our competitors have. The new products really need to stand out if we're going to put our flag in the ground."

"What about the clients?" asked Alex.

"I've got other client meetings before the end of the week. The team has more. I'll work with them to come up with some questions to ask. If I'm not on a sales call, the team will give me feedback and I'll make a point of going to see our top five clients specifically on this point. I think they'll appreciate being asked, aside from anything else."

"That's good," said Alex. "What about you, Heather?"

"Same as Michael. I'm going to look through all our recruitment material to make sure it's in line with the vision. I'm also going to speak to our recruitment agencies to make sure I know exactly how we're seen in the market. This recruitment freeze won't last forever.

I want them to be in the picture when we're ready to start hiring again, so we get the right people in."

"We'll be working on the messages together," said Kathryn, "but first we're going to survey the company so we're basing what we do on facts, not assumptions."

"In IT, we'll be supporting both streams by helping them get the best data for making decisions—or at least for testing theories," said Lee.

"All right," said Alex. "Our clients are the priority. I want you to test everything you do against what's going to be best for them. It's because of clients that I'm taking the employee angle to be a priority, too. People who feel their lives have been changed by Infinity are going to be much more open to the idea that we can do it for our clients. They'll be looking for new ways to do it. And to keep ourselves honest, especially our sales team, Michael, how will we know what we're doing is working?" He smiled at Michael, who was getting a mock consoling back pat from Kathryn.

"As it happens, I have no problem with honesty and being held to account," Michael said. "Sales is one of the most transparent parts of any business. Either you're selling or you're not. There's nowhere to hide. In this case, I'd say we'll know we've got our side of things on track when we can come to you with clear recommendations for products to scrap. And, we'll have the outline of products built with the vision and our clients in mind—products you can look at and say with confidence there's nothing like them on the market."

"For our part," said Heather, "we'll know we're on track when we're able to come back to you with a status report on what needs to be changed in our recruitment messages, based on what we've learned from recruiters and new hires. We'll also have the survey results of where we are now in relation to the promise of a life-changing employment. With that, we'll have recommendations on how to get from there to a place where we're living up to the vision."

"We've come a long way in a couple of days," said Alex. "I think it's definitely time to bring your teams into the picture. But I don't want you to come back just to me with recommendations. As a team, we have to stand by what we've decided. So, it's right that we present what we find back to this group for discussion. You've got a week, then we meet again."

Vision to Results Insights

The leadership team is starting to plot a strategy to take the organization in the direction of its vision of making life-changing investments for customers and for employees. They have recognized you can't plan a route to a destination unless you know the starting point as well as the end point.

Coming up with a strategy to achieve a vision requires:

1. A clear and honest view of reality—where you stand now. Whenever you can, it's better to make decisions based on facts and data rather than assumptions. For Alex and his team, this will include an employee survey and informatics about clients taken from their behavior on the website and their feedback to Infinity's call center.
2. There will almost always be too many things you can do. It's important to prioritize action. Infinity's executive team could be doing any number of things toward the vision but they leave the meeting clear on what's most important.

3. Alex's leadership team is not a cohesive unit, likely the result of a sustained period without clear direction. When people don't know what they're supposed to be doing, they often turn on each other. At least they're agreed that things aren't working the way they are and they've fallen in behind the vision. If they weren't agreed on the vision, getting anywhere at all would be difficult and would require some level of intervention or executive development.

4. Leaders should never create strategy for strategy's sake. Strategy should be created for customers' sake. Alex has been clear with his team that everything they present to him from now on needs to have been thought through in terms of the benefit to the client.

5. The focus areas agreed on have been written down and they're unambiguous. At the team's next meeting, there will be no room for anyone to say they didn't know their exact responsibilities. In our experience, limiting strategy to the key three to five core focal areas helps achieve this goal.

*　*　*

Chapter Three

Assessment

Heather already had a team meeting scheduled for that afternoon. Usually, she and her team used the time for each of them to report on the projects they were leading, and to discuss any particular problems that HR had been asked to advise on. Today, she intended to dispose of the agenda altogether, to focus entirely on sharing the vision and strategy with her whole team, and to ask them for their thoughts. If she was honest with herself, she hadn't been this excited about a team meeting for some time.

Infinity did not have a large HR team. The organization's philosophy was that HR should help set direction and provide human capital solutions for the business, and deliver competence development and training, but that managers should be responsible for their teams. It was not in line with Infinity's philosophy that HR should hold their hands in managing their people. Managers were expected to be able to lead.

Heather was the first to take her place at the circular table in the breakout room next to HR's area of Infinity's open-plan office. Pratik, the longest serving member of the team and Heather's de-facto deputy, arrived next and sat to her right. Karen, Veronique, and Andrea, the newest hire, came in behind him.

"Veronique, I know you were scheduled to report on the remuneration review today, but there's been a change of plan," Heather began. "I don't need to tell you Infinity's been in a bit of a holding pattern for a while now, but it's time to break out of that."

"It's felt a little less like a holding pattern than a downward spiral sometimes," said Pratik, looking over the top of his reading glasses.

"You know I've been meeting with Alex, Kathryn, and Michael over the last couple of days," said Heather, pushing on. "Together, we've set a direction for the company. It's one I think we in HR can find especially exciting."

Heather outlined what the leadership team had agreed upon, with particular emphasis on the part she saw HR playing in the promise of a life-changing shift for the Infinity team. As she finished, she spread her palms apart and looked around the table, with raised eyebrows.

"Are they serious?" asked Pratik. "We're going to offer life change? In these conditions?" Pratik had come

over recently from another of Infinity's offices. Heather had wanted to have him closer, to give some more depth to the head office team, but he had a tendency to see the glass as half empty. "I know things haven't been smooth recently, but that's been the economic reality. People know that, especially in our business," said Heather, swiveling her chair to look at Pratik as she spoke.

To her left, Veronique looked pensive. "In the last 12 months, we've closed an office and reduced the headcount in almost every team—"

"Not to mention sliced costs with a scythe whenever possible," Pratik cut in glad to have perceived an ally.

"Down to the bone, in some cases. We've had an almost total freeze on recruitment for six months."

"I'm the one who handles organizational design," continued Veronique. "I feel like I've been doing plenty of life changing for people recently and not for the better. I was the one who spent two months overseas helping close an office. That was 10 lives I changed right there."

"Like I said, I know things have been difficult, but that's the same for everyone in our industry," said Heather.

"But not everyone in the industry is planning to go out and offer quite such a rosy picture," said Pratik. "With respect, it seems deceptive."

Heather made a mental note that she would need to speak to Pratik privately. She valued diversity of thought in her team, but not divisiveness. People might have different ideas about the best way to get somewhere, but that was different from not wanting to get there in the first place.

"What do you think, Andrea?" said Heather, turning to the youngest member of the team. Andrea's enthusiasm was often a counterpart to Pratik's take on things.

"I can see what Pratik and Veronique are saying," said Andrea, with the diplomacy of someone twice her age. "I've taken my share of calls from managers needing advice on the procedures for letting people go. And I know many of them have found it hard to keep their teams motivated when they're doing the work of people who aren't here anymore."

"So you don't see any merit in what we're suggesting, either?" said Heather, starting to feel a little disheartened.

"No, I do," said Andrea. "I think we can root ourselves in the bad parts of what's been happening, or we can look at the good. I'd rather do that."

"What good?" asked Pratik. "Sure, I'm glad I'm still here, especially after moving my family halfway around the world. It's not like we haven't had to let people in HR go too, but is that really 'life-changing', not to have been made redundant?"

"But Pratik, you've been with Infinity for—what—seven years?" asked Andrea. Pratik nodded. "So it's been a while since you've worked anywhere else. Of course it's bad that we've had to let people go, and it's tough that we're doing more with less, but Infinity stands up incredibly well next to other places. Our competitors had to let people go as well and they're all cutting costs just like we are. I worked for an investment house that was going through exactly what Infinity has been through. I can tell you, it's better to work here."

"Thanks, Andrea," said Heather. "Veronique, do you really think we've got nothing more to offer?"

"I suppose Andrea has a point," said Veronique, leaning back in her chair. "I've never worked anywhere that put as much effort into getting the right culture.

Everywhere else I've worked, the focus has been on recruiting the guys who sell the most, or cut the most cost, or work the longest hours. You 'fit in' if you were the best at whatever technical measure they used for the job. You don't get a very rounded workforce that way and it makes for some unpleasant environments. I certainly wouldn't have been able to come back from maternity leave part-time in some of those places."

*   *   *

Michael was less confident than Heather as he went into his team meeting the following morning. Heather had the respect of the business because she had as firm a grip on financial reality as any HR person most of them had met. She worked in a field, however, that was more evolved. It recognized that some things couldn't be written on a P&L statement. Michael's team, however, lived and breathed the numbers. They were the ones who spoke to clients; they knew how everyone was doing; and the market gave them the most direct feedback possible: they bought or they didn't buy. There was no grey area there. Living by the numbers meant team meetings started early. No one on the sales team appreciated taking time out of the selling day to chat.

"I wouldn't say no to a life change," said Robert. He might have sported a ginger hipster beard, but he was one of Michael's most assertive sales people.

"For starters, I'll take the new system we were promised two years ago. You know, when the old system was only three years out of date. Anyone else up for it?"

"I'd like to see my targets shift down to something more realistic," said Rachel. "Everyone knows the market's softer than a hotel pillow. You can't tell me management couldn't see that coming when they set the targets. If I sell two thirds of my target this year, it'll have been a triumph. Where's the recognition for that?"

"Nobody is saying things have been easy, guys," said Michael.

"I should hope not," chimed in Jeremy. A veteran of the sales game, Jeremy's waistline was a casualty of long lunches past and—more recently—too many lunches at his desk in this more cutthroat world. "Some days, I walk out of here wondering if my dad wasn't right. At least if I'd gone into law, I could be riding the wave and handling bankruptcies and liquidations. That's where the boom is now."

"There are always going to be tough moments," said Michael, who was not used to being on a different page from his team. "But we have to prepare for the future. How are we going to be able to do that if we just shrug our shoulders and give up?"

"All right," said Robert, stroking his double chin, "but why now? The sorts of things you're talking about are the sorts of things customers have been telling us for years. We put all the feedback in the system. We report why sales don't happen or why customers ditch us for a competitor. We've known for a long time which products compare badly and which ones don't excite anyone."

"Robert's right," said Rachel. "I even put together a proposal last year for three new products that would do exactly what you're talking about. It never even got put on the table. There was no real consideration of it."

"So, you do think there are things that we can do?" asked Michael.

"I did," said Rachel, "but now I'm not sure."

"The guys in IT have been going through some of the data and they feel strongly there are things we can do," said Michael. "It turns out clients have been trying to tell us some things for quite a while."

"Such as?" said Matt and Darren together. The two salesmen were like long lost brothers. Both in their late twenties, both were born to sell. If it weren't for the fact that one was white and the other black, they could have been separated at birth.

Michael reached round behind him and grabbed a pile of bound printouts. He slid one across the table to each of the team. "Our friends in IT have done two things for us. First, they looked at the analytics from the website. You'll see there's a fairly big gap between the products where the customers spend the most time on the page and take the most action and the products where they spend hardly any time at all."

"So they're saying we've got products customers just aren't interested in?" said Rachel.

"Or we're not positioning them well enough for the customer to understand why they should be interested in them," said Jeremy.

"Exactly," said Michael.

"Exactly what?" said Rachel.

"We don't know," replied Michael. "We just know there's something there and we haven't been asking about it. It's time to start.

"And the other thing IT's done is look at the call center data?" said Jeremy, who'd been flipping ahead in the report.

"They took a sample couple of weeks and looked for trends," said Michael.

"And what did they find?" asked Darren, beating Michael to the punch this time.

"People are complaining after they've been sold things," said Michael.

"Why?" said Robert.

"Because we're selling them the wrong things," said Michael. "And it's going to stop."

*　*　*

After adjourning his team meeting, Michael walked round to the HR section of the floor. He caught Heather's eye and nodded his head towards the breakout room. Heather picked up her notepad and walked over.

"How was yours?" Michael asked, as Heather slid the door shut behind her.

"Pretty grim, to be honest. Yours?"

"Knowing my guys and yours, I'd say mine was probably grimmer," said Michael.

"At least they're not afraid to speak their minds," said Heather. "What have you said you're going to do next?"

"Rachel made some proposals last year that she felt were ignored, which is fair because they were. I've said I'll look at them again. I've also realized that I've gotten too far away from the frontline."

"What do you mean?"

"I'm the boss, so I get to choose my clients and I've had the same ones for years. I realize now that doesn't mean they're representative. I'm not in touch with what my guys are hearing or what they're saying."

"So what are you going to do about it?" said Heather.

"I knew Robert was unhappy but it wasn't till today that I saw just how frustrated he is. I'm going to go out with him when he meets his clients. I want to figure out what's us, what's them, and how we can do better. I am, as they say, exiting the bubble. What about you?"

"I've got a potentially disruptive influence in my team, too. I'm going to have a word with him and see if he'll come on board. I think you should do the same with Robert. Also, I've been talking to Kathryn and we've got an idea. It's something she's seen done elsewhere and she says it really works. It might be a bit out there, but by the sounds of it, we've both seen there's got to be a big shift. As a leadership team, I think we've lost some trust. Whatever we do next is going to have to be substantially different. We've got to send a signal."

"Are you going to tell me what this idea is?"

"Not right now, but soon. We've got a few things to do first."

*   *   *

One week to the day after they set their strategic direction, the leadership team met again. Kirsty stuck her head into Alex's office to tell him when everyone had arrived. Walking into the room, Alex noticed something was different. For a moment, he couldn't put his finger on it. Then it occurred to him: there was chatter in the room. For months, he realized, he'd been walking into total silence whenever the team met. Now, there was a buzz in the room.

The second change Alex noticed was that when he asked each of them in turn for their reports, more than one of them spoke to each point. Instead of operating independently, they'd been working together. Each had something to contribute to a discussion of each other's areas. In the past, eyes would have drifted to mobile phones when someone else was talking. Today, eyes were up.

Lee was the last to report, giving the group costs and schedules for each of their wish lists for upgrades to Infinity Investments' systems. When he finished, Alex thanked him and announced he had a final piece of business.

"After our last meeting, I asked Kathryn to do something for me. I wanted her to check that what we were talking about doing stood out as much as we thought. Kathryn?"

"Obviously lots of financial institutions make claims about clients having security and a better life for that," said Kathryn," which made this a big job, so I engaged an agency. They researched all the markets we operate in and could find nothing like this at the core of any competitor's offer, once you went beyond marketing slogans. We do have a genuine ability to stand out by realizing this vision."

"Something else I did after our last meeting," said Alex, "was call some of our larger clients, and some of the smaller ones, too. I wanted to test the idea with them. There wasn't much nuance in the feedback. They were all skeptical that this was just marketing. There's some trust we need to build. They also all agreed that, if we were serious, we'd definitely be out in front in terms of an attractive proposition."

"I've been asking at my sales meetings, too," said Michael, "and that's pretty much what I heard as well."

Alex continued, "I've asked Kathryn to use her communications skill to take what we talked about and distill it to be more granular, so we can give people a stronger flavor of what we mean when we talk about taking the company in this direction."

"Again I worked with an agency I've worked with before," said Kathryn. "They specialize in helping companies discover and define what their purpose is. Together, we created five pillars that sit underneath the vision of life-changing investments."

She pressed a button on her laptop and the screen at the end of the room came to life. In plain black lettering on a white screen were the words: "We grow most where we already prosper."

"Do you mean 'put the most effort in where we're already doing well'?" said Michael.

"That's exactly right," said Alex. "We want to grow everywhere but we have to have priorities. To get things started as quickly as possible, we're going to focus our efforts on the markets where we're already well regarded. It's going to be easier to excite those customers about the change. These are the best places to get over that initial suspicion I encountered."

"Makes sense to me," said Michael.

Kathryn moved to the next slide, which read, "We choose to make the biggest difference."

"We want to become known for being different," said Alex. "The fastest way to get there is for people to do our marketing for us by talking to other people about us. The more dramatic the difference we make in people's lives, the more they're going to talk about us. Given a choice between clients, we will choose the one for whom we can make the biggest difference."

"So we don't take your business if there's not a big change to make?" said Michael.

"That's not it," said Alex. "Again, it's about prioritizing. We're going to set our sights on clients for whom we'll make the greatest difference. That doesn't mean we'll be turning anyone else away. And if you don't like it, Michael, we can always work with you to refine it."

"No, that makes sense, too," said Michael. "We can't be all things to all people and we can't focus on everyone. It's good to have a frame."

This was going far better than Alex had expected.

"Lee, this is yours," said Kathryn, putting up the next slide. It read, "We use technology to give our people an edge and to help our customers change their lives."

"I like it," said Lee. "Technology has two different roles here. It's here to enable people at Infinity to do their jobs, but it's never going to change their lives."

"I've got some sales people who'd disagree," said Michael, thinking of Robert's complaints about outdated systems.

"It would change their work for the better," said Lee "It would make their jobs easier, but if a new sales system at work would be life changing for you, you need a different life."

"Got one for me?" said Heather.

"It just so happens…" said Kathryn pushing the arrow key on her laptop.

"We employ people who not only want change for themselves but for our clients," Heather read aloud from the screen. "That works for me. I can see that at the heart of recruitment, induction, training, and performance management. It's definitely a way to look at rising talent, too. If we're serious about this, it has to be the mindset of everyone who gets promoted."

As the discussion went on, Alex deliberately took more of a backseat. Where he'd previously had to run team meetings in a mode somewhere between chairman and ringmaster, this meeting almost didn't need him.

"There is a final pillar," he said. "We deliver an exceptional customer experience. It's not one that needs much explaining. If we can't do that, we're never going to be able to change anyone's life."

Vision to Results Insights

We have all been in the room when great ideas are conceived in great excitement. It's a wonderful feeling when that happens, but sometimes that feeling carries us too far. Giving the idea a reality check when you leave the room is a simple but effective way to make sure bad ideas don't survive. That's why the first part of VTR—Set Direction—includes three drivers that leaders should focus on to give them the best chance of delivering results: the vision, the strategy, and the assessment of the two.

Visions and strategies should always be assessed with team members, customers, and anyone who cares enough about your business to poke a hole in your ideas if they see a weak spot.

Alex and his team have talked to Infinity's clients about their vision. The feedback has been good: the clients would love to work with an organization that would change their lives. Clients have also confirmed Infinity's own research that they would be leaders in making such an offer. The feedback has also been negative: the clients are skeptical that Infinity means what it says. That's put the pressure on Infinity to work fast to build authenticity, credibility, and trust. When it goes public with the promise, it won't have long to show results.

Acting on the strategy will be easier, now that Alex has presented the team with Kathryn's ideas for making the strategy more granular. They have defined, for instance, that nothing short of exceptional customer service will achieve the strategy. When investing in getting to the next stage, this clarity about what's most important will help them make decisions about where to spend money and time.

By talking to employees about the vision and strategy, Alex's team has spotted a couple of potential disrupters in the business. Employees who are not on board with the new strategy might drag their feet, spread discontent, and work to undermine the work being done to execute on the strategy. It doesn't matter how many people in the boat are rowing in the same direction: one person rowing in the opposite direction, or not at all, can disrupt their efforts.

In short, having conceived a vision and a strategy, businesses need to pause in order to assess reality. This should include:

1. Checking that the strategy either puts them ahead of the trend or at least towards the front of the pack,
2. Making sure the strategy is something customers are behind and will give the business a competitive advantage,
3. Making sure there's enough granularity in the strategy that people can see what's going to make the most difference to delivering on it and make decisions about how to spend time and resources accordingly, and
4. Checking within the business to spot people who could slow things down.

*   *   *

Part Two
Engage & Excite

Chapter Four

Believability

The email arrived at 9 a.m. on Wednesday. The subject line read "Invitation" and the message in that followed was only slightly more illuminating. "You are invited to contribute to a change," it read. "Your voice matters and your presence is expected on Monday morning at 8:30 sharp." It went on to give an address in an up-and-coming area of town. The recipients weren't able to see who else had been invited. The invitation was signed "Alex," which meant whatever other questions the recipients had, 'Should we go?' was not one of them.

* * *

Shortly before 8:30 on Monday morning, Andrea from HR found herself standing outside a red brick building with whitewashed double doors set in an arch about twice as tall as she was. In less fashionable times, it might have been a warehouse or perhaps a garage.

Soon afterwards, she spotted Robert from sales coming round the corner, a leather satchel over his shoulder. They were quickly joined by Jeremy, Veronique, Pratik, and a few of Kathryn's communications team who had shared a cab. There were a couple of assistants Andrea recognized from other floors, and a guy from accounts she remembered because he'd once quizzed her about a travel expense claim. In all, she counted 15 people waiting outside the whitewashed doors. Those who did not know each other made quick introductions and soon found out no one knew any more than they did about the mysterious invitation.

Just as Jeremy pulled out his phone to check the time, one of the whitewashed doors opened and Alex Dalton stepped out, dressed in jeans and a blazer over an open-necked light blue shirt. With a welcoming smile and sweep of his arm, the CEO invited them in. They stepped into a high-ceilinged space with glossy white walls and a variety of office chairs, tables, and more comfortable seats arranged in clusters around the room. In one corner, a young man in black-rimmed glasses and casual jacket was making a coffee for himself in a kitchen area.

Alex moved to the opposite end of the space. The words "LIFE CHANGING" were spelled out behind him in freestanding letters that came up to his waist. He cleared his throat.

"First, thank you all for coming," he said. "By now, you've all been told that my executive team and I have

set a new vision for Infinity. From now on, we are in the business of changing lives with the investments we make. As members of the Infinity team, you make an investment in us and we want you to be better off for it. And our clients trust us with their money, so we certainly want them to be better off for that trust—much better off. We want to stand out by being the investment house that offers products that change their lives, too."

A few of his audience shifted in their seats. Alex had asked his team to be sure to invite those who'd greeted the new plans enthusiastically and who would make good role models in the new approach. He'd also asked them to invite anyone who'd had strong reservations. He'd gone through Heather's, Michael's, and Kathryn's suggestions meticulously, rejecting several of their first choices because they included too many senior people. He knew that for Infinity to shift gears, everyone needed to feel listened to and part of the change. He had insisted that the final 15 needed to be drawn from across all parts of Infinity. Several on the list had flown in from other offices. He wanted a broad perspective for this meeting, but he also wanted their feedback on whether the exercise should be repeated in all the Infinity offices.

"I know some of you are having a hard time with this," he continued. "As Infinity's CEO, it's my job to set the direction along with my team, but we know we're not on the frontline of the changes—you are. What we decide has to work for you, and no one knows better than you do what that means in terms of effort. I've asked you here today because I need your help. As a leadership team, we have decided that Infinity needs to differentiate itself." Alex threw out his arm to indicate Michael, Kathryn, and Heather, who were sitting in a semicircle behind him.

"I want you to know we acknowledge that a change like this brings uncertainty," Alex went on. "We can't tell you exactly what this change will bring or what it will mean to individuals. We're still in the process of working out what it is. Today, you're very much part of that process. I can only tell you two things. First, we are here to help you. Second, I know we can do it," Alex went on. "What I see in two years' time is us asking our clients what it means to be with Infinity and being told that choosing Infinity changed their lives. And when we ask the people who work here the same question, they will say the same thing."

There were many folded arms in the room, Alex noticed, but several people were taking notes and it was only the beginning of the day.

"This session is happening out of the office because what we're doing is not everyday. We're not working *at* Infinity Investments right now, we're working *on* Infinity Investments. We're asking what it's going to take to get us to the point where clients and employees say,

'This is a life-changing company.' What do we need to do? What do we need to stop doing?"

Alex paused and put his hands together. He looked around the room, inviting comment, but nobody spoke. Alex looked from person to person, waiting for someone to speak. He struggled to keep his face from giving away his feelings. He knew this change couldn't come only from the top, and if he couldn't get a pilot group of 15 to believe in what he was trying to do, how would he convince the whole company?

Eventually, Robert broke the silence from the back row. "Look, don't get me wrong, I like the idea of changing people's lives. Who wouldn't? But how are we expected to do that when it feels like we're hanging on by our fingertips some days?"

Until this point, no one had paid much attention to the quiet man in the casual jacket, but he attracted their attention now as he pulled out a marker pen from a collection on a small table. He took the cap off and strolled over to shiny blank wall behind Alex. He began to draw a man clinging to the edge of a cliff. Beads of sweat dripped from the cartoon figure's knotted brow.

"I should explain that David is going to be our note taker today," said Kathryn, getting up from her seat and coming to stand at Alex's right elbow. "His job is to interpret what you say. Sometimes the picture is clearer when it's… er… a picture."

David responded by drawing an ornate picture frame with "Life-Changing Investments" written inside it in red.

"It's a good question, Robert, and it's the question that today is about answering," said Alex. "Is that how everyone else feels?"

"My team's already heard me say this, but I just helped close an overseas office," said Veronique. "I changed people's lives by making them worse."

David began drawing a coffin in black on the wall. There were a couple of snorts around the room. David smiled over his shoulder.

"All right, it wasn't quite as bad as that," said Veronique, sitting back into her chair and allowing herself a smile. "I know some of them have gone onto other jobs. One of them connected with me on LinkedIn last week and, actually, it looks like she's taken a step up."

"I do hear you," said Alex. "It's no secret we've been in a tight spot, but it's only by changing the way we do things that we're going to get out of that spot. It's a hoary cliché, but what doesn't kill us makes us stronger. Couldn't that be true here?"

Behind him, David was rapidly altering his coffin to show a grinning body sitting up with a hand weight in each fist.

"This does seem to be taking a somewhat macabre turn," said Robert. "This isn't 'The Walking Dead'."

"I should hope not," said Alex, laughing and quietly relieved that things were taking a positive turn.

"And we're not in the ground yet, which is not to say Jeremy couldn't do with a go on those weights," Robert added.

"Charming," said Jeremy, giving his right bicep a mock squeeze. "It's all muscle, you know."

"Maybe we have tendency to focus on the downside," cut in Rachel. "Sure, there's life in the old dog yet, as long as we're on clichés and life and death metaphors. But there are some serious problems, too."

"Rachel's right," said Robert. "Respectfully, Alex, it's okay for everyone to get together in a conference room and frame a pretty slogan on the whiteboard—no offence David—but, like you said, they're not the ones who actually have to make it happen."

"We're under resourced, and we don't have the systems we need to do this," said Jeremy.

"It's true," said Alex. "We have asked you to do more with less. What I'm hoping will come from today are ideas about how we can do less with more. What I mean is: stopping is as important, maybe more important, than starting. We haven't been able to give you what you needed because we've been stretched thin. This morning, you're going to hear from each member of my team about what they see is the vision for Infinity for their areas. That's going to include stopping doing things that don't fit. Stopping those things could well free up resources to give you what you need to do the right things. Can I ask you to keep an open mind as you hear from them this morning?"

There were nods of agreement around the room.

"And above all, I need you to contribute," Alex continued. "We're not saying we have all the answers. We're genuinely looking for suggestions."

More nods. Alex felt himself breathing deeper. They were getting somewhere.

"But I don't want to mislead you." Alex felt the group sit up a little. "We need your help to realize our vision and execute on our strategy, so we do want your advice on how we can make that happen. That's where we're at, though. The vision and strategy are set. The five pillars that you've all seen are what we're going to be focusing on. We will be putting most of our resources into the markets where we're already successful. If we have to choose between the most profitable clients and the ones for whom we can make the biggest changes, we will be choosing the latter. We will not be investing in technology just so we have the best systems. We will have the systems you need. For our clients, however, we might well have the best technology, because that's going to contribute to how we change their lives. We will invest in giving them the best experiences and we will only employ people who share this vision. It's important you understand that."

"You're saying we're out if we don't like it," said Robert.

"I'm saying we hope to persuade you that this is the best thing for Infinity in the long run, even if the short term is hard," said Alex. "But if I can't persuade you of that, let me ask you a question. Why would you work for a company that was going somewhere you didn't want to go? You're a talented salesman, Robert. You could go anywhere. For your own sake, it should be somewhere you're happy."

Kathryn, who had remained standing, said, "I'd like to make an observation, if you don't mind, Alex. What I'm hearing is a high level of frustration, and people only get frustrated when they care. Is that right?"

"Yeah, I think that's true," said Jeremy. "I care, and I like the picture you're painting. I guess I just don't see a way to make it more than a picture."

"And that's why we're here," said Heather, standing up and moving next to Kathryn. Alex stepped back and took a seat next to Michael.

"It's time to roll up our sleeves and work that out as a team," continued the HR director, "but I thought, first, it might be helpful to tell a story."

Heather reached down to a table at the end of the front row of seats and picked up a remote control. She pressed a button, and the lights in the room dimmed as an LCD screen unfolded from the ceiling.

The picture on the screen showed a baby in a smart-looking incubator. It could have been the set of any hospital show on TV.

"Jeremy is right that having the right equipment is essential to do a difficult job properly," said Heather. "We know what the tools we need are, and we expect to have them if we're going to do what people expect of us. If we're not given the right stuff, people need to expect less of us. Right?"

She looked around the room where heads were bobbing in agreement. "Except, in some situations, expecting less would mean accepting the absolute worst," Heather went on.

She explained to the group that the incubator in the picture on the screen cost $40,000. "So you might think the reason infant mortality rates are high in some less well off countries is that they don't have expensive equipment. The truth is that wealthy countries donate medical equipment all over the world, including incubators, but within five years, 96 percent of them are in equipment graveyards."

She advanced the slideshow to a picture of an incubator outside in a dusty hospital parking lot. "Can anyone guess how a state-of the-art incubator ends up like this, in just five years?" she asked.

"Because they don't know how to use it properly?" offered Jeremy.

"No," said Darren, whose family was originally from Kenya and who had spent two years teaching there after university, "that wouldn't be it."

"That's right. Incubators are much less complicated than they look," said Heather. "Mostly, they're just about keeping the baby warm and cozy. They're not hard to control."

"There's no electricity?" suggested Rachel.

"It's a good guess, but the real reason is they break down all the time. Here, too. The difference is we have people who know how to fix them. They aren't complicated to use, but they are complicated to fix."

A new slide showed side-by-side pictures of two car engines. On the left was a photograph of the workings of a top-of-the-line European car. It looked as if a stylish collection of matt black boxes had been snapped together under the direction of an interior designer. The car on the right had an engine made of tubes and cables wound into a dirty spaghetti. Henry Ford would have recognized it as an engine. He might have thought the other was from a spaceship.

"You don't see many people in their driveways with their heads in the engine anymore. You need a specialist mechanic. The car on the right, though, is a car any mechanic could fix. It's an old Toyota 4Runner, and you'll find them pretty much anywhere you go in the world. That means you'll find spare-parts and people who know what to do with them."

The photographs on the screen slid sideways to reveal a pair of car headlights poking through a wooden cutout, and wired to a car battery.

"That's how some smart people came to make an incubator pretty much entirely from bits of a Toyota. The bassinet sits on top and the headlights create warmth. You don't even need a manual to fix it, you just need to know how to replace a headlight."

There was a murmur of appreciation around the room for the kind of lateral thinking needed to build an incubator from spare car parts. Heather handed the remote control to Alex as she walked back to her seat, and he got up to stand in front of the group. He pressed the power button. The screen folded back into the roof and the lights came back up.

"We don't always have everything we need, but that doesn't have to stop us," Alex said, making eye contact with each person in front of him. "So let's use today to look at where we are, where we need to get to, and what we really need to make that happen. Ready?"

*   *   *

For the rest of the day, each member of Alex's team painted a picture of their area of operations. They shared their ideas for shifting the work their teams did to align to the vision of Infinity as a company that boldly set out to be different. They talked about what the leadership team meant by making life-changing investments for clients and in the people who worked there. It was all captured by David, who worked his way around the walls of the room as the stories took shape.

Michael, looking relaxed in a blue polo shirt, talked about the need to go through all the company's products and check whether they delivered on the promise to be life changing for the people who bought them. He filled the group in on the preliminary feedback he'd had from clients. He also told them that Infinity would be adopting and embedding the Net Promoter Approach so that they could track and score different customer segments, different offers, and different teams in the quest to deliver an exceptional experience for Infinity's clients.

"We're just going to be asking clients how likely they'd be to recommend us to someone else," he explained. "It's nothing to be afraid of. If they wouldn't recommend us, they wouldn't recommend us whether we asked them or not. It's better that we have a chance to ask them why, so we can do better."

He finished by challenging them to break into smaller groups and approach the product question as a client would. What products would they like to see? What would change their lives?

Alex had insisted on the latter part of the session. Michael had argued it was a waste of time to think a randomly selected group, drawn from all over the company, could possibly come up with better ideas than his team of specialists who talked to clients every day. By the end of the session, however, he had committed to taking three ideas that came from the group back to his team to see how they could be developed. What Alex had noticed most from walking around the room during the discussion was how engaged Robert had been. Alex couldn't hear everything being said in the groups, such was the level of noise in the room, but the ideas had seemed to be pouring out of Robert.

Kathryn took over from Michael, using her time to talk about the importance of listening to Infinity's clients. She reported on what she and her team would be doing to capture the voice of the customer, and to make sure everyone in Infinity was hearing what clients had to say. The exercise she asked everyone in the room to do was to think how they could make sure no decision was made by their teams until they had considered how it would affect the client, and how it would contribute to Infinity reaching that point where people were saying that their decision to go with Infinity had indeed been a 'life-changing' move.

At the end of her session, Kathryn asked if anyone had any questions.

"I have one," said Robert. "If we're truly serious about seeing everything from the client's point of view…"

"We are," said Alex, disappointed that he seemed to have been wrong about Robert coming round.

"Why not appoint a CXO?" continued Robert.

Alex felt his shoulders drop. *People never ceased to surprise you,* he thought. "I'll have to take it to the board," he said, "but I think that's an excellent idea."

*   *   *

Heather's portion of the day happened after the lunch break and involved little talking by Heather herself. She began by breaking the room into three groups and asking Kathryn, Alex, and Michael to sit with one group each. She wanted the groups to talk about their experiences working for Infinity, and to divide those experiences into what was good, what was bad, what could be improved, and which of those things could be described as making a decision to work for Infinity as 'life-changing.'

Heather herself spent time listening to each group. While there was diversity in their experiences and ideas, their energy was the same. People ignited with enthusiasm when asked to design their ideal workplace but what they wanted from Infinity was neither extravagant nor beyond the ability of Infinity to provide. No one was asking for Xboxes in the kitchen areas or extra weeks of holidays. Everyone in the room wanted to do a good job and, as Kathryn had noted, their frustrations arose when they felt they were being unreasonably stopped from doing it well.

There were certainly differences in focus. Members of her own team felt that changing the culture of Infinity was the highest priority in achieving the vision, while most of the sales team argued that new systems and products needed to come first. But nobody was arguing that change wasn't possible. When asked to step up and contribute, no one was saying it couldn't be done.

David and his marker pens were kept busy as each group fed back to the room what they thought was needed to take Alex and his team's vision for the company, and engineer it into the DNA of Infinity.

As Heather's session drew to a close, Alex stepped back to the front of the room. Chairs scraped as the groups unfurled from their huddles to face the CEO.

"I couldn't be more delighted by the way today has gone," Alex started. "Everyone one of you has contributed and, if we can bring this much energy back to Infinity and multiply it by the number of colleagues who aren't here today, I have no doubt we will achieve all we want to achieve."

"And more!" Robert called out from near the back of the room. His sentiment was met with much agreement.

"There have been some great ideas coming from everyone," said Alex. "What I want us to do now is look at those ideas we've got up here on the wall and rank them. I'd like each of you to take a piece of paper and give each of the ideas two scores. I want you to give a score out of 100 for how much impact you think the idea will have on getting us to our vision, and a score out of 10 for how much effort you think it will take to execute the idea."

When they'd made their notes, they handed their papers to Michael and took a short break. He entered their scores into a spreadsheet he'd been preparing as the ideas were conceived during the day. He took the average score out of 100 for the impact of each idea, and divided it by the average score out of 10 for the effort it would take. Then he sorted the spreadsheet, so the ideas with the highest final score were at the top.

"What we have here," said Michael, as the group studied the results on the LCD screen, "is an average score for each idea, taking into account its potential impact and how easy it would be to implement: the greater the impact and easier the implementation, the higher the score. But that's just to give us a starting point. What we'd like to do now is to look at that list and decide what's right, and where the weighting has skewed the idea too high or too low."

"We're going to leave here," Alex joined in, "with a list of things we're going to do and a priority level for each one. This plan belongs to all of us, so I want to make sure you agree with it."

For the next thirty minutes, the group went back and forth, debating what should be given greater emphasis and what had been given too great a priority. The exercises highlighted the different lenses in the room. Those from HR again put weight on changing the people in the company, and those from sales argued for changing the products. The accountant Andrea had recognized at the beginning of the day made the cogent argument that almost no one had properly thought about cost when considering the effort some ideas would take to implement.

"I'm not sure we're going to get everyone on the same page," said Heather, leaning in to talk into Alex's ear as they watched from the side of the room, while Michael facilitated the group conversation.

"I'm not so sure," said Alex, leaning back in his chair. "They've all got different perspectives. That's to be expected, but have you noticed what's changed since we started this morning? They're listening to each other. They're actually acknowledging that someone else might have a point. It's starting to feel like we've got a team here."

*   *   *

At four o'clock, the group was taking the final break of the day. They were standing around the small kitchen area, finishing the sandwiches and pastries brought in at lunchtime from a fashionable patisserie around the corner. Kathryn and David came out of a back room carrying two boxes, which they put down in front of the group. David pulled back the cardboard flaps and started handing out smaller boxes to each of the group.

"Everyone, we're going to be breaking this up soon," said Alex. "It's been pretty clear to me that there's real excitement here about what we can do to take Infinity to a new place. But it's also fair to say, not all of you felt that way when we started this morning. And that means you have colleagues who are going to need to be persuaded that we've got it right."

"You want us to sell the vision to them?" asked Robert.

"No, not 'sell'," said Alex. "I want you to do what we've done today. To talk about it. To ask the questions."

"And to film it?" said Rachel, looking at the box David had just handed her.

"I know you've all got phones with video cameras already," said Kathryn, "but we've put together some kits. It's a phone preloaded with video apps and you'll see there's a little lapel mic that plugs into the headphone socket. We want people to sound good as well as look good. If you haven't shot a video on a phone before, you'll find the kit is pretty easy to use, even if you're not Scorsese."

"I'm more a Tarantino girl, myself," said Rachel, pulling the phone from its box and pointing it at the last croissant, "specifically *Pulp Fiction*. You call that a Royale with Cheese?"

"Then yours is going to be a particularly interesting film to watch," said Kathryn, "because, as you have gathered, this isn't just a party gift. You are indeed going to be making films."

"Short ones, I hope," said Robert, good-humoredly. "I think we've all seen that Jeremy hasn't got much of an attention span. He's the only person in the world who likes the ads on TV. He thinks they're tiny little shows."

Jeremy coughed, a doughnut halfway to his mouth. "Bloody powdered sugar."

"Yes, short ones," agreed Kathryn. "As Alex says, what we want you to do is to take what we've talked about today, and ask your colleagues what they think of the same questions we've been answering. What does the phrase 'life-changing investments' mean to them? What do they think it would it look like for clients, if we were the firm that offered life-changing investments? Ask them why they work here, why they choose to work here. We want you to ask them what they think we need to stop doing and what we need to defend. You record the results, and the multitalented multimedia David will do the rest. Let's split into groups again and we'll have a practice."

Rachel tilted her camera from the snack table to Jeremy. "Whose motorcycle is this?"

Jeremy looked straight down the barrel of the lens, holding up a pastry, and gave her his best Bruce Willis impression, "It's a croissant, baby."

Vision to Results Insights

It's much harder to persuade people to come on a journey with you if they don't believe you'll ever get there. Infinity's offsite is about helping people to believe that it is possible for the organization to lift itself out of the recent slump and realize its vision.

Communication about change on this scale needs to be heard above the "noise" of everyday work life. Pulling people out of the office to something a bit mysterious and a little different has done that in this case. It might not be possible for all of Infinity's employees to experience the same, which is where capturing the key points in a visual story and handing out video kits come in. The group of 15 who attended this offsite now has a chance to spread the word by engaging in a version of what they've experienced at the offsite: sharing the visual change story or narrative, asking people what they think about the direction of the organization, and talking to them about the hurdles that they'll find on the way. What they produce will be different from anything employees have seen before, so it will also cut through the "noise."

Leaders need to make it clear that they will help employees navigate the uncertainty that comes with change. At the same time, they need to be firm about what is expected of employees. Alex, for instance, has left Robert in no doubt that his views will be listened to; but that there won't be much of a future for him at Infinity if he doesn't believe in the direction the organization is taking. If Robert's objections can't be reconciled with Infinity's strategy that will be a difficult conversation, but it's one that will need to take place. When an organization's leadership is clear about its intentions, there are no surprises, and people can make decisions for themselves about whether the fit it still right.

Change is emotional and leaders need to keep checking with employees. They won't always be able to have special events like Infinity's offsite, so they should be checking on a day-to-day basis. It doesn't have to be more complicated than asking, "How are you feeling?"

In this chapter, what Infinity is demonstrating about ensuring the wider organization believes in the strategy is:

1. Leaders need to set the stage for change across all levels of the organization and make it clear that they are there to help.
2. Communication about fundamentals like vision and strategy needs to stand out from the background noise.
3. The organization's expectations of what will change needs to be clear to everyone.
4. Leaders should look for bright spots in the organization—Alex asks his team to invite people who are already looking like role models for the organization Infinity wants to be.

*   *   *

Chapter Five

Desirability

The metallic clink of a ballpoint pen tapping a water glass stopped the chatter on the floor.

"Thank you, everyone. Thank you for coming," said Alex, looking at the majority of Infinity's head office team standing around their desks or resting against windowsills, the city falling away behind them. There was just room towards the front for a few more on chairs.

"Thank you for squeezing in. We could have taken this offsite, but I didn't want that kind of formality. Right now, we have a shared project that we're working on, and this is where we're doing it. So this is where I want to talk about it."

Just behind him, to his right, stood his leadership team.

"Between us, Kathryn, Heather, Michael, and I are going to be holding meetings like this in all our offices. As CEO, I'm doing as many as I can, but this is a collective effort. We're all responsible for the changes that need to be made. And I'm including all of you in that. It's not something I could just expect you to do; it's something you have to want to do, and I'm glad you do." He waved his arm to indicate the TV screens on the walls around the room. "Michael, could you get the lights?"

The people in the room immediately recognized the face on the screen. Julia worked at Infinity's main reception desk. She'd been filmed by Rachel, standing in the lobby first thing in the morning, with a stream of people arriving for work behind her.

"What do I think about working somewhere that changes people's lives?" Julia said into the camera. "I think that's exactly what we should be doing. My dad had to give up work to look after my mum. He had income protection but it didn't last. She had insurance, but it didn't cover what she needed it to cover. I'd love to think I worked for a company that made sure none of its customers had to go through what my parents went through."

The scene changed to one of the meeting rooms on the sales floor. Matt and Darren, two of Infinity's most successful salespeople, sat at the opposite end of the table from the camera. In the background, through the glass wall, people were working the phones at their desks.

"So, what do you think of the vision thing?" Robert was asking off camera.

"I think we all know I could sell sand to camels," said Matt, stroking his goatee.

"Just not as much of it as I could," cut in Darren, grinning.

The video zoomed in on Matt, briefly losing focus but regaining it as he said, "But sometimes, the thing is, you do want to believe in what you're selling. It's not all the same."

Robert panned the camera phone to Darren, now looking more serious. "Yeah, what he said. Just because we work in finance, doesn't mean we have to, you know, check any kind of values at the door, does it?"

The video cut to Samira Ansari, from Kathryn Chivers' communications team. Andrea had caught her at her desk. Her free-spirited long hair was tied back in a contained avalanche.

"So, what do you need to make it happen?" Andrea's voice was asking.

"If we're serious about it, we need it to be a filter. We need to be allowed to look at what we're doing, and be allowed to stop doing it if it doesn't make sense. If it's just a slogan, that's no good. It needs to be a question we ask all the time, about everything. Is this going to help us make life-changing investments? Everyone has to have permission to ask that question."

Back in the sales floor meeting room, Matt and Darren had also been asked what they needed.

"There's no question about it. I need Darren to up his figures," said Matt, deadpan, and the two threw back their heads laughing and nearly fell off their chairs.

The scene dissolved to an Infinity logo with the words "Life-changing investments" incorporated underneath it. Michael flipped the lights back on.

"I'll be honest with you," said Alex, when the murmuring had died down. "Not so long ago, I wasn't all that excited about coming to work. Some days, I didn't really know what it was all for. Did the world really need us? What made us any different from any of the hundreds of other options that our clients had? I believe the direction we've all set answers those questions. Today, I'm excited about coming to work every morning. When people ask me what I do, I'm excited to tell them. I hope you are too."

There were pockets of applause around the room.

"It isn't going to be easy. Change isn't easy. Adapting isn't easy. What is easy is sitting around doing the same things, waiting to be overtaken and to become unnecessary. All of you will be sitting down with your teams and working out exactly what the changes we need will mean for you.

"But I can tell you now that the big picture—of what it means for you—is a company you can be proud to work for, and a company that is going to go from strength to strength. Don't forget: we're not just talking about making life-changing investments for our clients. We're talking about making life-changing investments in our people. We're going to make sure Infinity is a company people want to work for because it's a company that makes being here worthwhile. This will be a company that helps people make the most of their careers without them having to give up the other things that matter to them.

"There is going to be change, but I know you're ready. You've told me you're ready. Your time, as they say on the gameshows, starts now."

There was more applause this time, but what pleased Alex most, as he walked across the floor in the direction of his office, was how many nods he'd seen around the room as he was talking. He knew he'd had the attention of everyone there. Teams grouped around desks in animated conversation. There was a palpable energy on the floor.

"We're ready," he heard someone say as he walked past.

* * *

Heather had fallen into step behind Alex as he headed for his office. She walked in behind him.

"Alex, if you've got a moment, I'd like to talk to you about something," she said.

"Sure. Kirsty will be in if I've got anything, no doubt," he said, gesturing to the sofa and the armchair that sat in the corner of his office. "Sit down. That went well, don't you think?"

"I do," said Heather, "but reluctant as I am to sound like Michael, I think it's only going to get us so far."

"You think hearts and minds are one thing, but wallets have a vote, too?"

"That's exactly what I think. We were never going to make any changes if we didn't have people believing in what we're doing but to keep ourselves to that vision is going to take monitoring. We have to build it into our DNA. I'm not saying performance measures and bonuses are the answer to everything. That's the last thing I think, but we certainly can't have them working against what we're trying to do."

"What gets measured gets done?" said Alex.

"It'll always be that way. Bonuses, job descriptions, promotions... they all send important signals about what we value."

"I agree," said Alex. "Do you have a suggestion?"

"We need to do two things. We need to introduce a measure to the bonus structure that recognizes alignment to the vision and the strategy of the company. We can't just reward making money. We have to reward doing it in a way that helps us be the company we need to be."

"Can we do that in the existing structure?"

"I think we might. I've got Pratik working on it."

"Has he warmed to the new way of doing things at all?" asked Alex.

"We had a good talk. Pratik is like an oil tanker. It takes a long time but he can change direction."

"But sometimes he needs a tug boat?"

"Something like that," said Heather, laughing.

"What's the second thing?"

"Bonuses aren't the only reward for doing well. There's promotion, too. We need to be sure we're promoting people who are good examples to others of what we're looking for."

"These are good thoughts, Heather. I look forward to hearing what Pratik thinks and, yes, I think you should update the career framework to make compatibility with our goals an essential feature of any promotion. In fact, I think you should go one step further and have managers start sending you the names of people who fit that description so we can make sure they're getting the development they need."

Heather stood up to leave, but Alex gestured for her to sit down again.

"There's one other thing I'd like you to consider. We're making this change for our clients, so I want their voice in all these decisions. We're going to start using the Net Promoter score. It's a simple but powerful approach and links directly to our aim of delivering exceptional customer experiences. I want you to factor that into the frameworks, too."

"I'll get the oil tanker on it," said Heather and they both laughed.

Vision to Results Insights

In the last chapter, we talked about how important it is that employees believe a change is possible for the organization and, most importantly, for them personally. But that's only half the battle when it comes to capturing the hearts and minds of employees. They also have to want the change. If your employees believe you can change but don't want you to, you're still not going to get where you need to go. The videos Infinity's change agents have been making are about sparking the fifth element of the VTR framework: Desirability. People will work hard to bring about a change they want even when it's difficult to do.

And, of course, that effort should be rewarded, which is why Heather is looking at how Infinity pays and promotes its people. Having the wrong behavior rewarded and poor role models rising through the organization will, at best, hinder a culture change but is more likely to kill it altogether.

Leaders need to:

1. Make sure the individual's economic interests are aligned with the interests of the organization—don't recognize or reward people for working against what you want;

2. Know who your top talent are and make sure they're getting what they need, especially what they need to champion your change; and

3. Measure culture, which could be through a formal survey of employees (quantitative) or organizing facilitated focus groups (qualitative). It might start with asking your customers what their current experiences are. If your customers aren't feeling your culture the way they should be, you know something is amiss and you can dig deeper.

* * *

Chapter Six

Communication

Scott drove to and from the airport almost every day, but he'd never lost his awe of a A380 screaming over the windshield in its last few hundred meters to the runway. If ever man had made something that did not look like it was meant to stay in the air, it was the Airbus.

"How was the trip?" he asked his passenger, after the impossibly large plane had flown over.

Alex Dalton was in the back seat, wearing jeans and an open-necked white shirt that showed off a slight tan.

"I learned more in the last week than I have in a long time," said Alex. "That was one of the most useful things I've done since I became CEO."

"I would have thought you'd have spent more than enough time on the phone in your job, Mr. Dalton."

"There's a lot of talking but not enough of it to the right people, Scott," said Alex. "A couple of days in a call center, though. Then you're talking to the right people."

"Did you take a few days off? See the sights?"

"No, I spent the rest of the time walking the floors, talking to people, dropping in on meetings."

"I bet that put people on their toes," laughed Scott.

"Maybe at first, but after a while they open up," said Alex. "And then they start asking the questions they've not been sure they're allowed to ask."

*   *   *

A month earlier, Alex had received an email, not to his main account but to the special feedback account he'd had IT setup. The videos that had been made after the offsite had inspired him to do it. Seeing so many people telling their stories and giving their reactions to his vision had brought home to him how few people in the company he actually spoke to. He realized how much his view of the company was filtered through the people who reported on it to him.

He had published the email in his monthly update on the intranet and also in the newsletters that clients received. One of the first emails he received was from an employee at Infinity's call center:

Hi, Mr. Dalton,

Thank you for inviting us to write to you.

Every day, I talk to customers about policies and products that are developed by people I have never met in an office I have never been to.

We enjoyed everyone's videos about making life-changing investments. We made some of our own here—I made one, myself. Did you see any of them? We didn't get any feedback, so we weren't sure if our videos were only shown here. It's a big change and I know I'm not the only one who has questions about what it means.

The customers I speak to see me as Infinity Investment because I am the one who speaks to them on behalf of the company. Sometimes, when I'm explaining something to them, I wonder what they would think if they knew how cut off we really are from what we're talking to them about.

I have worked here for two years now and don't know of anyone from head office ever coming here. My boss has been here longer and she doesn't think it's happened in her time either. I know her boss goes over there two or three times a year.

I made my video about the vision because I believe in it. I enjoy working here. I just wish I felt a bit more connected to what's going on.

Yours,

Ali

* * *

Alex read the email out at his next executive team meeting. "Have any of you been over there?" he asked.

"Veronique has been over a few times," said Heather, "for team restructures and things like that."

"There are no sales people there," said Michael, shrugging his shoulders, "so, to be honest, it's never occurred to me."

"What about communications?" asked Alex. "It's a back office, but it's not a small office. How do we include them?"

"Well, they have the same access to the intranet as everyone else," said Kathryn, "and if they need specific support, they call Samira. She has responsibility for that office."

"But she doesn't go there?" asked Alex.

"No," said Kathryn, adjusting her scarf. "It hasn't seemed necessary."

"As you'd expect for a call center, there's a fair-sized IT team there," said Lee. "Their manager comes over here a few times a year for training and some of the bigger meetings. But I haven't been myself."

"I can't say too much because it hasn't occurred to me to go there either," said Alex, "but that was a mistake. I've asked Kirsty to find a week in my diary to go over."

"A week?" said Michael.

"For a start, I'm going to spend a few days on the phones myself," said Alex. "Ali's right about what he says in his email. They answer all day for decisions we make. I want to hear for myself what customers think."

"But a week?" said Michael.

"Like any of our offices, I can work anywhere I can plug in," said Alex. "It's not going to make a difference to the people I email or whose papers I'm reading if I'm somewhere else for a week, but I realize how important it is to be seen and for people to know they can talk to us. Kathryn, you're going to get Samira to let people know why I'm there. I want people to see we are listening and we're open to the feedback."

"I get it," said Michael. "It does sound like a good idea."

"I'm glad you think so," said Alex, "because Kirsty is looking at your diary, too."

"Mine?"

"Like the man said: they answer for decisions made by people they've never met. Most of the time, those questions are about products that ultimately you're responsible for."

"What time is Michael's first shift on the phones going to be?" said Lee. "I think I'd definitely like to call then."

"I wouldn't call before you've had your turn," said Alex, which cut short the laughter at Michael's expense. "This email isn't the only one like it that I've had. As a team, we all need to be seen and we all need to spend some time listening, particularly to people we don't usually get a chance to talk to."

"Is there a plan for this?" asked Lee.

"There's going to be," said Alex. "We've moved pretty fast from agreeing on a vision and a strategy through to working with everybody to get their backing. Everything is still feeling new and the pace of change is still high. But now that we've accepted that this is where we're going, we need to get things formalized."

"You're right. We've moved quickly and communications has been playing catch-up," said Kathryn. "I'm going to get my team on this. We'll work out exactly what messages need to go out, when, how, and who is going to give them."

"We need some guiding principles," said Heather. "From what Alex is saying, honesty is one of them and visibility of leadership is another. Is that something we're agreed on?"

There were nods of agreement around the room.

"Right," said Alex, "it's time Michael and I got fitted for our headsets. Let's see what we learn because we're going to use that when we get together again to talk about how we're going to communicate better with clients."

Vision to Results Insights

After Believability and Desirability, Communication is the final driver of the second element of the VTR framework: Engage & Excite.

Communication is fundamental to success in business. Infinity Investments has not done a bad job when it comes to communication with the wider team. As soon as the executive team decided on a vision and a strategy, they tested it with their teams. They created a visual narrative of the change story captured from their offsite (which has now also been placed into their recruitment and induction process). They've even made change agent videos and we have the impression that the executive team has continued to talk, share, and connect with the wider audience of the whole organization.

We know they've been talking to clients, too, but only selected clients for the purposes of assessing the vision and determining what needed to be done to execute it. There's been no proper planning for communicating and marketing the change to customers. It's an easy mistake to make when you're feeling your way and aren't quite sure how you're going to do things. But uncertainty is best addressed up front rather than avoided as a topic. When we don't talk about things, people fill in the gaps for themselves.

When a change asks a lot of people, it's especially important to make sure they understand they're valued and appreciated. That's a message that should infuse all messages.

In summary, there are a number of things an organization should be doing:

1. Planning. Communication takes discipline, which is where Infinity has fallen down—communication has been ad hoc and responsive rather than planned and proactive. The organization needs a matrix: who should they be communicating with; who should be doing the communicating; and in what media. These days, that requires thinking about social media, too.

2. Internally, leaders need to be in constant, open conversation with the whole organization. Alex had started the ball rolling by setting up a feedback email address, but he obviously hadn't sufficiently encouraged his

team to follow his lead in being more visibly open to feedback.

3. Uncertainty should be the primary target of communication. People are more confident when they know what's happening, why it's happening, and what it means for them. If you don't know, it's better to tell them you don't know than to have them assume you do know but you're just not telling them.

4. When it comes to something as all encompassing as organizational strategy, communication should be coming from the leaders. That means from the executive team but also from every leader and manager at line level. Visibility and transparency are key.

* * *

Part Three
Enable & Execute

Chapter Seven

Action Roadmap

"It's only been a short time, but it feels like we've come a long way," Heather said to her team the next day, warming her hands round an actual mug of coffee for a change, rather than a paper cup. They were meeting around the bench table that was the centerpiece of a coffee shop a block from Infinity. Heather had wanted them out of the office to signal they'd be shifting again from their usual routine. Following their leader's example, Veronique, Andrea, and Karen all had large coffees in front of them. Pratik had stuck to his usual Earl Grey and was engrossed in dragging the tea bag around the mug.

"I think we can all agree that Andrea, Veronique, and everyone else made a great video," Heather went on. "I hope you're as inspired as I am by the potential we're looking at."

"I have to say, I found it a bit humbling," said Veronique, reaching up and adjusting the stem of her glasses. "You know, I went to that offsite more than a little skeptical. We just seemed to have been on down cycle after down cycle. I was expecting a lot of waffle, a bit of time drumming in a circle, and generally, a light coat of paint splashed on to conceal the problems. The fact is, I walked out of there really tuned back in. It was a little inspiring to be in a room with people who went in with totally certainty it could be done. Andrea, you were one of them. So, thanks." She raised her coffee mug in Andrea's direction.

"Hear, hear," said Karen, raising her mug to join the toast. "I thought it was brilliant."

"You're very welcome," said Andrea, acknowledging the salute with a nod and tilt of her coffee, "but I know it was easier for me than you, Veronique. I haven't been at the sharp end as much as you have. For my part, I think you and some of the others made a valuable contribution by keeping the conversation real. Let's be honest, if we want to change the company, we've got to admit there are structural problems. And you're right, you can't fix those with a coat of paint. This is going to take hard work, and there's no point wearing rose-tinted glasses. There are some things we have to face up to."

"That's all true, but you might need to ease up on the metaphors," said Karen, and the four women laughed. Pratik pulled his teabag from the mug and put it on a saucer.

"Structure is exactly why we're here," said Heather, holding her hands up. She was delighted with how things were going. Veronique was known for her professional reserve, something reflected in her uniform of roll neck sweaters set off with pearls. And Pratik might not have fully embraced the new ways of doing things at Infinity but he was no longer sniping at everything, which Heather saw as a good sign.

"At the offsite, we all agreed that working on the culture of Infinity was essential to the change, so we gave it a high priority," she went on. "That was in broad terms. It's up to us, today, to decide what we're going to do to specifically make the changes we need to transform the culture. And when I say 'we,' I mean it. But if there are things you think I should be doing as the leader, I want you to tell me."

"I know I complained before about the recruitment freeze," said Pratik, speaking for the first time. "Now, I think it's a good thing. I think the first thing we need to do is to rework our recruitment framework. If we don't hire people who buy into Infinity's vision, we're never going to get there."

"Sure," said Veronique. "I don't disagree, but we turn over 15 to 20 percent of our staff a year. First, we've got to get that number down. If we can do that, recruitment will be less important because we'll be recruiting fewer people. With respect, though, it's also less important even if it stayed as high as it is."

"I'm with Veronique," said Karen. "Even with a 20 percent turnover, 80 percent of us are still here at the end of every year. If we want to change the culture, we have to change the way the 80 percent see the world."

Heather had noticed Karen speaking up more in meetings since Infinity Investments had embarked on its new strategy. Karen clearly no longer doubted she had a valuable contribution to make. *There was one life already changed*, Heather thought.

"What are you suggesting, Karen?" asked Heather.

"I think we need to look at our training and development, for everyone who's already working here. Are we giving leaders the right skills to get these changes spread through the company? Do they know what our employee value proposition is? I think we need to benchmark our engagement, so we know what drives the performance of the people who work here. Only with that, and some proper surveying, can we can find out really what our people see as the life-changing investments we're making in them."

"On the subject of investments, we have to look at how we're rewarding people," said Andrea. "We've been pretty traditional until now. Any kind of bonus is based on performance. Like a lot of the industry, we're about paying you for what you do, not how you do it. If we want a culture that feels different—one where we're making people feel we value them, and that we're investing in them—we're going to have to look at incorporating behavioral considerations into the bonus calculation. If you do more than you're asked to do, but you do it in a way that doesn't align with our values or the financial services regulator, you don't get a big pat on the back."

"Sounds like just a couple of days' work then," said Pratik, smiling and raising his eyebrows ironically. "Just as well it's not urgent."

"Come on, Pratik, even you must see that's a good idea," said Veronique. Pratik looked hurt.

"Pratik's kidding," said Heather. "I've actually had him looking at how we pay and reward people for a little while now. Obviously, it's a sensitive topic, which is why he's been doing it quietly."

"Sorry, Pratik," said Veronique.

"We're going to need a bit of time to get used to it if you're going to start making jokes now, Pratik," said Andrea, smiling at him. This time even Pratik laughed.

"Pratik did hit on something I wanted to emphasize," said Heather. "Looking at how we reward people is urgent, but more than that, it's important. In the sorts of changes we're trying to make here, it can be easy to mix up the two. We need to be sure what we're spending time on is important, not just urgent."

"Do you feel there's something we've been talking about that isn't important?" asked Veronique.

"Not at all," said Heather. "I've been really pleased by the way this team has kept its eye on the big picture.

I haven't heard any of you say one thing that isn't important, but we can't do all of them at once. That means we've got to pick the most important from the list and work on them first."

"We went through a recruitment framework adjustment not so long ago," said Pratik. "I've still got all the material. That's something we could do quickly."

"We made two decisions at the executive level when deciding our vision was life-changing investments," said Heather. "We decided what that meant for our clients and our employees. But they're not equally crucial. The business is going to get more stuck if we can't find a better way to be for our clients. I agree with Veronique that we've got the best chance of moving that needle fastest if we focus on the majority of Infinity's people. And that means those who are already here."

"You want me to work up some ideas for keeping the cultural change rolling through the company?" said Veronique.

"I do, but I think the more important thing is the work Pratik is doing on how we pay people and what we give bonuses for," said Heather. "We've all been here long enough to know that nothing is going to make a bigger change in a shorter period of time than that. It's the clearest signal we can send that this change is structural and meant to last."

"What we need is an action roadmap," said Karen, opening the cover of her notebook and snapping her pen into life.

"Great idea," said Heather. "Get down that our first priority is the remuneration framework. You can put me down for the next action on that. I'm going to take Pratik's work to the leadership team. We can't decide to change the remuneration framework in HR. We need to get the leadership team onboard, especially Michael. I'll do that and come back to you when I have their agreement, assuming I get it."

"Okay," said Karen. "Assuming you do get a green light to go ahead, what should I put down as the way we'll measure whether a change in the pay structure is working?"

"Let's make our first metric of success whether managers comply with the new framework," said Heather. "We'll audit samples of performance reviews to make sure managers are taking into consideration all the things they should be when giving bonuses, not just doing it for the same reasons."

Heather waited for Karen to finish writing before continuing. "Veronique, I want you, Karen, and Andrea to work with the communications team on defining our employee value proposition. Kathryn's team is working on their priorities right now. Part of that is going to be making sure our message is getting out. We should make sure that message includes what it means to work here.

Let's make sure what we're saying is consistent with what our people say they value. We don't want it based on assumptions. Also, I've agreed with Kathryn that our potential hires are part of the audience we're trying to reach. We can use her team's skills and the work they're going to be doing to start incorporating messages into what we're saying to future colleagues when the freeze is lifted. In terms of an action roadmap, that's surveying first, and then using that feedback to formalize the employee value proposition. We'll rework the recruitment framework later."

Again, she waited until Karen had finished writing. "Karen, please note in the roadmap that the next report on all of these things is due at our next meeting. At that point, I want you all to be able to talk me through the steps you're going to go through and the timeframes."

*   *   *

Kathryn Chivers's team was responsible for external and internal communications. Piet Hurkman headed up the public relations side, helped by a manager in each of Infinity's major offices. Samira Ansari, who had featured in Andrea's video about life-changing investments, had two assistants and ran Infinity's internal communications from the head office. Her role was global but she stayed in touch with regional managers and local concerns, mostly by video conference but with the occasional trip for face-to-face meetings.

"It's a big shift for the market," Piet said, when the three sat down to map out their roles in realizing the new vision. "We know it's not how we're seen currently. We have a good reputation, especially after coming out of the last few years with no allegations of bad practice, but it's a leap from there to get people to see us as the company changing lives."

"Do you think it's as big a leap internally, Samira?" asked Kathryn.

"It's definitely a leap. People are proud to work here, but I wouldn't say they see what they're doing as changing client's lives," said Samira. "But the good news is, I think it will be easier for them to see Infinity as changing their own lives. Every team here would have someone who came here because we've got a reputation as a better place to work. When people leave Infinity, it's generally not because they don't like working here."

"We have to make a plan," said Kathryn, leaning forward, "and we have to make a big impact quickly. Where do you think we should start?"

"We can go big, advertise, run a serious campaign about our changes," said Piet, gesturing towards the row of TV screens tuned to various 24-hour news channels. "I think we could have a major impact. We could combine that with a social media element. We could maybe take some of those video snippets, polish them up a bit, put them in our YouTube channel, and cross-promote them on LinkedIn. People will connect to a human face on the company. If they can see that we believe in what we're saying, they're more likely to believe it's real."

"The executive team has talked about supporting this with advertising," said Kathryn. "If we're going to advertise, we want to advertise the specifics. Michael and his sales and product teams have already met to work out what they're going to focus on in the next three months. They're going to be coming up with just what we're going to be offering that stands out. From now on, our messaging needs to be about being crystal clear with our clients. Part of what we can do that's different from the competition is to give it to them straight and in plain English. We won't be able to do that yet, so I don't want to go big just at the moment."

"In that case, what about getting Alex on the road?" asked Piet. "It's obvious he feels strongly about what we're doing and it is genuinely a new direction. That's something he can talk about right now. There are media opportunities and speaking opportunities for someone in his position in the industry who is willing to talk about shaking things up in the industry."

"Agreed," said Kathryn. "I'll talk to him about it when we meet this afternoon. What about internally?"

"We saw at the town hall meeting how well people responded to the stories in those videos," said Samira. "Like I said before, there's a good understanding internally that we change lives for employees. There's more to do but it seems more important we focus on showing people how we change lives for clients. If our own people don't believe we're life-changing for customers, we're never going to persuade customers that's how we're different."

"That's definitely our priority," said Kathryn. "We weren't that good at it before, but now everything has to be looked at from the customer's point of view first."

"I think we need to look for clients who can talk about the difference Infinity has made to their lives," Samira went on. "It'll take some time to put together, especially as that wasn't something we were looking for before, but those stories are definitely out there even without the new things that Michael's working on. We just have to find them."

"That's a good start," said Kathryn, "but we need to cast our net wider than just those with a good story to tell. If we're going to be in the business of investing to change lives, we need the best possible understanding of what those lives are."

"We need focus groups and individual conversations," said Piet. "I'll put together a plan for market research and a budget."

"That's good, but we've missing a step," said Kathryn.

"What's that?" asked Piet.

"Things have happened quickly and Alex got things off to a good start by talking to as many people face-to-face as possible. We talked about this in the last executive team meeting. We're doing well as teams in following up on the new direction, and for our team that has meant a lot of scrambling."

"You can say that again," said Piet.

"We certainly found ourselves playing catch-up," said Samira.

"And, what that's meant is that we've been reactive. We haven't made a proper plan," said Kathryn. "We got caught up in the moment but now we need to step back and make a plan to keep the strategy and the change visible. We need to find a way to maintain the sense of urgency."

"We need a campaign about the strategy itself," said Samira.

"Exactly," said Kathryn. "I want you to come up with a way in which people are reminded every day that things are changing. And, I want them to be able to see progress. A goal is more meaningful if it's in sight. Coming up with that plan and executing it is our number one priority. I expect us all to take responsibility for that."

"You know those thermometers they use for fundraising?" said Pratik. "We could have something like that. Every team is agreeing on targets. Let's encourage them to put those targets up there, along with the milestones they'll need to pass. That will show how close they are to reaching their goals and what they've achieved along the way."

"What if I asked all the teams what their most important metric of change is? We could have a combined chart we updated monthly," said Samira. "We put it up where everyone can see it, so everyone can track not only their team's progress but Infinity's progress as a whole company. Like a dashboard."

"People love to see a gauge move from red through orange to green," said Kathryn. "Let's start there. We get the vision and the strategy where people can't miss them, and we make sure their measures are up on display, too, along with color coding. We get Alex out there, setting the scene in the market. And then, Samira, you can start rolling out the next phase with some customer feedback."

* * *

"So, Michael, you've split your team in two," said Alex.

The leadership team was back in the boardroom, where they'd begun to set the vision only a few weeks ago.

"That's right. The Red Team is looking at what we should stop selling, or what we need to rebuild to fit. The Blue Team is working with the product guys to come up with new offers."

"If the Red Team is about stopping things, shouldn't the other team be green for 'go'?" asked Kathryn.

"See, Kathryn, that's always been your problem: not thinking outside the box. Blue Team is working on blue sky thinking. I think Heather needs to get you on a creativity program. Then maybe you could finally live your dream and get out of corporate communications and into sales."

One of first things Alex had noticed coming with the new vision was a more relaxed dynamic in his leadership team. They'd gotten along all right before, some of them better than others, but even the stronger relationships could be prickly. People, he'd noticed, were much more defensive when they didn't know exactly what they were supposed to be doing.

"Kathryn's team's been quite creative with this speaking circuit they're putting me on," said Alex, standing up and walking towards the window. "I know that getting the message out is important, and this is a great first step, but I don't want to send the wrong message."

"We're working on key messages and the right audiences. We'll have all of that for you," said Kathryn.

"It's not that. I don't want to send the message out there that Infinity is some sort of one-person operation," Alex said, looking out of the window. "I might have started this company, but I want people to know that this is a place where teams thrive. They should know there are all sorts of good leaders pushing through top-class initiatives in every area of the company. This is a place of opportunities for the people who work here, a place where good ideas are listened to wherever they come from."

"I see what you mean," said Kathryn. "And it's better for clients to feel there's a big team behind what we're doing."

"We wouldn't want anyone to think it's all going to end up pear-shaped if the founder falls under a bus," said Michael.

"Thank you, as ever, Michael, for your keen use of imagery. I shall try to stay away from buses. Regardless, Infinity isn't a one-man business. It's a team and as such I want us all out there talking about what's happening here."

"Okay, I'll have Piet rework the schedule and cast the net wider for opportunities for us all to speak in our areas of expertise."

"Other than that, your team's absolutely on the right track with the activities you've highlighted in the communications plan, Kathryn. Once we make our vision and our strategy part of everyone's day-to-day work, we can rollout further phases to cascade and keep moving it deeper. I particularly like the idea of putting messages about our clients front and center when we're ready. I also like the plan Piet's put together for market research. Once Michael's been through and added his comments, I think you should go ahead on that, in concert with his team."

"It's a dream come true, Kathryn. You really do get to work in sales," said Michael, grinning at the head of communications who was pretending not to notice.

"Now, Heather, I think remuneration is next on the agenda," said Alex.

"Yours, Heather?" asked Michael, on a roll now.

"Yes, I suppose, in a way. Mine and everyone else's, including yours."

"I'm not sure I like the sound of this," said Michael, pushing back slightly in his chair.

"I think you'd better explain," said Alex, walking back from the window and taking his seat.

"If we want this change to be more than skin deep…"

"Which we do," added Alex.

"Then we have to make the change at the foundation," Heather continued. "We have to make sure that people who are doing the right things are recognized. If we keep rewarding people in the old way, we'll keep them doing the old things."

"What do you mean by that?" asked Michael, leaning forward and putting his elbows on the table. "My guys sell, and the more they sell, the more they make. It's not an 'old' way; it's the way it works. Why muck around with it?"

"Because it didn't work," said Heather, "or at least it won't work to get people to start thinking the way we need them to. If every sale counts just the same, people will make every sale they can."

"Precisely," said Michael, clapping his hands together. "That's exactly what the bonus system is there to ensure."

"Yes, but what if what they sell isn't the right product for that customer?" said Heather. "You can make a sale that's great for the salesman but not great for the customer. That's not the vision. We need to encourage longer-term thinking. Satisfied customers come back; delighted customers come back more. That's good for salespeople in the long run."

"And that means it's better for Infinity," said Alex. "I see your point, Heather."

"How are we going to measure whether we're selling the right things?" said Michael, throwing his hands up.

"That's where you come in," said Heather. "I want Veronique to work with your team. We know this has to work for them, and it still has to be an incentive. So let's work on it together."

"Suddenly everyone wants to work with me," said Michael. "I know sales is the center of the universe but—"

"That sounds like a sensible plan," said Alex, cutting in. "Ultimately, we're not changing the business we're in. We're still in financial services. We're still about selling, and we're still about making a profit. We need to give the sales team an incentive, but what we choose to reward is going to have an impact, probably the biggest impact on how successfully we change."

"And how fast," added Kathryn.

"Given how quickly we need to turn that around, I think all your teams have done a great job of picking the most important things to work on," said Alex. "Our job as a team now is to look at where we can use our influence to get things happening faster. Some roadblocks only get cleared when you're working on them from the top, as well as head-on."

Alex fanned out several sheets of copy paper on the table in front of him, one for each of his direct reports and the action roadmaps they'd agreed with their teams.

"On each of these," he said, "we know there's something we can contribute as a team. We're going to do two things now. You're going to look through each other's action roadmaps and see where you can get involved in making things easier. There's obvious overlap in many of these areas and you bring complementary skills to the task at hand. Then we're going to take copies of everything, so you can each tell your teams exactly what's going on with other teams so they can consider that as they go about their own work. But you're not just going to print out the list and share it. You need to be able to put it in context for your team. What does a change somewhere else mean for them, and for the clients? You can look at these as separate lists, but that's not how I see them. They're all parts of a single roadmap, as far as I'm concerned, and that roadmap is our responsibility as a team. I'm holding us jointly accountable for all of it. But today, we've identified the biggest battles."

"The first is to find out what customers want," said Michael, "and getting our products right. We need some level of predicative analytics and market research. Without that, we're nowhere."

"It's not as easy to separate the ingredients in the soup as that," said Kathryn. "There are lots of things we've got to get right or it won't work. We have to get the message out there to the market. If no one knows we're doing things differently, it's not going to make any difference"

"And we have to have the right people working here, with the right incentives to make the difference," said Heather.

"Exactly right," said Alex. "Those three things are our greatest priorities at the moment, and I'm glad to see you feel as passionately about them as I do."

*   *   *

Over the following weeks, the signs of change became more visible. People walked out of team meetings carrying large pieces of paper with headlines like "First 100 Days," which they stuck to the walls around their team areas. The more creatively inclined people drew their goals as cartoons, while in some departments the posters were more likely to take the form of charts and bulleted lists. Almost everybody had a copy of their team's plan-on-a-page pinned next to their computer monitors. Often, they had highlighted those parts that applied most specifically to them individually.

The computer monitors themselves carried reminders too. Samira arranged with IT for a rotating screensaver, with screen captures from the internal video serving as backgrounds for quotations from the interviewee. She herself appeared in one, with the words "Permission to make a difference" next to a screen capture from the video Andrea had made of her.

In the second week, Alex made good on his promise to take his message to the whole company. He'd appeared in two webinars, timed to allow teams to participate wherever they were in the world. He had talked about what Infinity was learning about its customers from the market research, and what feedback he and his team had in response to the presentations and interviews they'd given. An email had gone out before the webinars. It invited questions and included a facility to ask them anonymously, if necessary. As well as filling everyone in on progress, Alex had answered all the questions he'd received as fully as he was able. Where he wasn't in a position to answer a question, he'd still acknowledged and explained why he couldn't be more forthcoming.

Afterwards, Samira had called the leaders in every office, and had talked to members of her informal network. The word from both groups was that people appreciated the openness.

"It feels as if we're doing something together, for once, rather than having things done to us," one of Samira's contacts had told her. Not everyone was feeling that way, however, as Heather would soon learn.

Vision to Results Insights

Alex and his team have moved through the first two sections of the Vision to Results framework. They have set a compelling direction for Infinity and begun the process of organizational engagement through effective communication and involvement.

Infinity Investments is, conveniently, working its way through our VTR model from start to finish, in a linear fashion. First, set a direction with a vision and a strategy you've assessed for reality. Second, engage and excite by making sure your people believe in the direction, want to go in that direction, and are being communicated to in a way that provides clarity and a dose of motivation.

In reality, the framework is a loop. A business might, for instance, have a great direction and a team that is completely onboard but nothing is happening. When that business looks to VTR for an answer, we might see its problem is in execution and that's where we would start to work with them.

Enable & Execute, the third stage of the VTR framework, is where Infinity Investments finds itself now. It begins with laying out an Action Roadmap. The company's strategy tells the business, in broad terms, how it is going to get from where it is to where the vision puts it. Within that, however, detailed plans need to be made.

In another nod to the messy reality in which we all operate, it's a good idea to think of action roadmaps as being written in pencil. The world changes and that can happen quickly. It would be foolish to stick to specific goals or metrics that no longer make sense in changed circumstances. It would be equally foolish, however, to have no plans at all. As we have seen in Infinity's story, having no plan means you're drifting. It's still possible to reach a destination by drifting, but relying on sheer luck is no way to manage an organization any more than throwing a message in a bottle into the sea is a way to deliver letters.

Action roadmaps should:

- Focus on the next 12 months—they should be realistic and based on what you can reasonably foresee.
- Concentrate on what is important not just what's urgent. We've seen in our story that some at Infinity think the answer to the

problems of the organization lie in upgrading some of its software. To them that's urgent, but it isn't in Infinity's case anywhere near as important as some of the more fundamental, customer-facing changes that need to be made.

- Show what is important and what is most important. Leadership teams need to be clear on this with their teams. Any organization or team can only do so much at one time, so it needs always to be doing what's most important. In Infinity's case, they have to demonstrate trust and convince their customers that they're different. That gives them an excellent filter for deciding where effort most needs to be spent.

*   *   *

Chapter Eight

Capability

The following day, Michael stood in the doorway of Heather's office, waiting for her to finish a phone call. The HR team all had their heads down, looking busy. If he was honest, he'd always been skeptical of HR people. In other jobs, the only qualification to be in HR had seemed to be the ability get under his feet while completely avoiding doing anything actually useful. His first real meeting with Heather outside Alex's leadership team meetings had been about two months into his time with Infinity. He'd needed to find out Infinity's procedure for replacing an under-performing sales manager. He hadn't expected much, but that was the other thing about HR people: you couldn't avoid dealing with them.

"It depends," Heather had told him.

"On what?" he'd asked, expecting her to shovel a binder full of forms in his direction.

"What's best for the business," she'd said. "We make sure it's handled properly, but you're running the team. You make the decisions and we'll work with you to get the best results."

Even though they hadn't always seen eye-to-eye since then, he had to admit he valued her opinion. But only if he were asked at gunpoint.

Heather put down the phone and raised her eyebrows in his direction.

"Coffee?" he said.

*   *   *

There was a cafe on an upper level of the building, with stunning views of the city. Infinity's management favored the cafe because it was less formal than a meeting room but the thick carpets and low voices still kept things fairly confidential. The cafe was busy when they arrived, but they found a table by the floor-to-ceiling windows.

"My guys aren't up to it," said Michael, as soon as they'd sat down, "not as it stands."

"Would this be the Red Team or the Sky Blue Team?" asked Heather, a playful twinkle in her eyes.

"It's not the product side. We didn't have a tough time at a high level deciding which products to kill, and we've had good ideas for new products. The problem is matching the product to the customer."

"How so?" asked Heather.

"I've been out every day this week with our sales managers. I've taken a back seat; I wanted to see how they ran with the new focus."

"From the pained look on your face, I'm taking it they didn't run very far."

"It was a train wreck. Most of it anyway. I've spent a week listening to them babble about how big we are, how we have global market coverage, our history of amazing returns, blah, blah, blah."

"Nothing about the new products?"

"Plenty about the new products: a tedious abundance about the new products, in fact—and perhaps a little too much about the old products as well."

"So what exactly is the problem?"

"They don't ask any questions. They don't stop talking long enough to listen to what the customer needs. I hadn't realized it before. Their inability to listen was masked, but it's startlingly apparent now we've changed things."

"What do you mean it was masked?"

"Before, we were selling pretty much the same thing as everyone else. You didn't need to ask the customer questions. Our product x was not so very different from someone else's product y. The customers knew what was on offer, so they weren't really choosing between us and someone else on the basis of the product. But we've met the new brief; we have highly differentiated products and a commitment to matching the customer to the product. We can't do that if we're treating the customers as all the same. We have to get to know them better and we have to be able to tell them how our products are different and better for them."

"Isn't it still all sales, though?" asked Heather. "Listening to the customer's needs, framing the product as a solution?"

"Yes, it is," said Michael.

"So what were your sales guys doing before?"

"From what I can gather now, they were walking into meetings with the options and relying on existing relationships and what the customer knew about us already. Now we have to paint a picture of the vision for the customer and these guys don't have what it takes to do that. They're flat. They're not able to tailor a pitch to a particular customer, if you can even call what they're doing pitching. It's more like putting the menu on the table and standing there till the customer has chosen between the fish and the chicken. I bet if I phoned half these clients today, they would not tell me they walked out of those meetings understanding that we're doing something completely new. Our guys didn't bring enough heat to those meetings to take the edge off an ice cube."

"What do you want to do about it?"

"It's obvious I need to get more involved. But I need your help as well."

"Say that again," said Heather. "I liked hearing it."

"I'd like one of your team to work with me to profile the whole sales organization. I want to work out where their strengths are, and what we can do to develop them. It's clear there needs to be some training, but I think it's likely that there are going to be some on the team who aren't going to be able to make the jump. The only way to sell the new Infinity is to embody it yourself. You're never going to convince a customer you're in the business of changing lives when you are demonstrably uninterested in the customer as anything more than a leg up to your next bonus."

"If we can't change the people, we need to change the people," said Heather.

"That's right, sensei," said Alex, nodding and taking a sip of black coffee. "There's no turning back now."

* * *

Over the following couple of weeks, Karen spent time with the sales team. She went to their meetings, she went on sales calls, and she had meetings with each of them individually. Darren called her the team's embedded HR person and Jeremy suggested she get herself a flak jacket with "HR" in white letters on the front.

When she felt she had gathered enough information, she met Heather in her office.

"What's the gist of it?" asked Heather, as she put the folder with Karen's findings on the glass desk between them.

"It was a good reminder that just because people do the same job doesn't mean they're the same type of person," said Karen. "You've also got a wide range of experience in there. Jeremy's been doing this forever but Darren, Robert, and the others are relatively new. So you've got at least one person who knows much more than the others—"

"Which comes with the downside that their views are more likely to be set in stone," said Heather, finishing Karen's thought for her.

"That's right," said Karen.

"How are they going about aligning what they do to the new direction?"

"I'm not really sure they are," said Karen, "which, to be fair to them, isn't that surprising."

"Why?" said Heather.

"They live by the numbers and die by the numbers. Their processes aren't complicated or sophisticated. You join the team, you make calls, your sales are tallied, and your performance is assessed accordingly. We're asking them to make massive changes at every level of what they do. They need to know much more about the products they're selling and much more about the clients they're selling them to."

"And that takes insight and the ability to build trust, and to make connections on a deeper level," said Heather.

"It does, but first they have to be convinced that it makes sense. As they've never been measured on those skills before, it's not coming naturally that a win is more than a sale. They don't yet see that for a sale to be a win, it has to be a definite win for the customer too. That's certainly within the job description for sales in some industries, but it's not been part of the job description here before."

"Are they getting any guidance from Michael?" asked Heather.

"Not from Michael so much as from Alex," said Karen.

"Alex?" asked Heather, raising her eyebrows.

"Yes, he was in a lot of the sales meetings I went to and he came out on some of the sales calls. It was Alex talking about the new direction. Michael didn't really have a lot to say about it."

"And did you come up with any recommendations?" asked Heather.

*   *   *

"We want to start a sales academy," said Heather, when the agenda turned to sales at the next executive team meeting.

"Interesting," said Alex. "What exactly do you have in mind?"

"We put the sales team on a six month program," said Michael, who had liked Karen's idea as soon as Heather and Karen had described it to him. "We start with mindset. Some of the team has bought more into the idea of viewing sales from a customer perspective than other people on the team. We need everyone starting from the same point."

"And if they can't reach that point?" asked Lee.

"I think it can only go one of two ways," said Michael. "They either see that doing things this way is best in the long run for the company and for them, or they see that this is the way the company is going and decide this isn't where they should be."

"This will be rolled out at the same time as the new reward structure," said Heather, "so it will be clear that this will be how sales will be measured from now on. You won't be able to ignore it and carry on as you have been."

"Not if you want to get paid the same," said Michael.

"The most important thing is we're giving everyone a chance," said Alex. "This is a radical shift and it's not in line with a life-changing culture for employees to take a sink-or-swim approach. We employed people to do one job, now we're asking them to do another. It's appropriate we offer support."

"Karen's profiled the whole team," said Heather. "The academy is going be tailored to a range of needs. The idea is: we work to everyone's strengths rather than trying to force everyone into a single mold. There's room for different approaches, provided the goal is the same and the customer experience is great."

"One thing the team does have in common is a competitive streak," said Michael.

"Really?" said Kathryn, with mock surprise.

"So we're planning on introducing gamification as part of the engagement and competence development solution," said Heather.

"I thought sales was already a big game," said Kathryn.

"It's the game of life, Kathryn," said Michael, "but, seriously, there's an easy way to keep score in sales, which is what we've been doing. What we're going to do is broaden the way we keep score to reflect the wider view we're taking of what we reward people for. Lee, do you want to cover the details?"

"I've got a programmer on my team who has had some experience with this," said Lee. "He's come up with this great idea. We're going to take everyone's sales performances, combine them with metrics like their net promoter scores, and then color code them."

"Gold for the best performers, silver for the next, and so on," Michael said, his excitement palpable.

"And, those colors are reflected in their profile picture on the intranet or on the phone display when they're calling someone internally," said Lee.

"What do you mean?" asked Kathryn.

"Profile pictures on the intranet will have a colored border, and so will the picture that shows up on your display when someone's calling you," said Michael, coming in again. "When you get a call from a salesman of my caliber—"

"It comes up blank?" said Kathryn, to general laughter.

"I think you get the idea," said Lee. "By combining the metrics to give an overall score, we're not giving too much specific information about an individual to anyone. It's an aggregate ranking, so your sales might be down this month but your net promoter score might be through the roof, so you're still gold.

"That way, you're still in the game even if your sales are down, because your sales might be down because you actually showed a customer why a particular product wasn't actually right for them. They're much more likely to say they'll recommend a salesman who's that honest. As we've said all along, we should be rewarding that.

"And, by including the net promoter score this way, the sales team has a positive incentive to remember to ask the question at the end of a call or a meeting. It's been a struggle to get them to do that up to now."

"Both sound like great ideas to me," said Alex.

"Let the games begin," said Kathryn.

Vision to Results Insights

The power of the VTR framework does not come from any of its elements being obscure or unexpected. The ability of the framework to effect profound change lies in the combination of all the elements and the fact that we developed the model as a result of years of working with hundreds of companies. In that practice, we saw that few companies have all the elements working at the same time and none do it by accident.

It's hardly surprising that capability is on the list. You can't be successful if your people aren't capable of doing what it takes for your company to be successful. In the case of Infinity, it recruited and rewarded sales people for their sales numbers. Those who were able to sell the most—regardless of its fit to the customer who bought it—were those who were most successful. Salespeople who didn't operate that way—or who didn't appreciate an environment of sales at any cost—would likely not stay.

By setting a new vision and changing direction, Infinity has created a need across the organization for at least some—probably most—employees to have a different mindset. They also need new skills. Michael's sales team needs to be able to profile their customers on more dimensions than the customers' budgets and willingness to buy. The team has to know how to understand the customer's needs and what will make that customer most likely to recommend Infinity to someone else.

Infinity will not achieve this by imaging a single archetype of an ideal salesperson and then trying to twist and contort every salesperson they have into that mold. They need to work to people's strengths. If someone's strengths will never align to what Infinity needs from them, it's better for both parties that the salesperson finds somewhere their strengths are needed.

The idea of gamification is both new and not new—companies have had league tables, employees of the month, and sales awards since what seem like the dawn of time. But technology has made much more sophisticated things possible. It's one of the most exciting developments we've seen and the results of gamification on the speed and depth of corporate competence development can be astounding when it's done right.

Gamification is especially powerful in developing a "learning organization"—one that follows a win, learn, change model. When you want to do better in a game, you have a compelling reason to spend some time studying how you're doing, how other people are doing, and thinking about what you could do better.

When looking at capability, therefore, you should:

- Assess individuals' knowledge, skills, mindset and processes;
- Take a strength-based approach; and
- Connect the development solutions you choose to deploy to the strategy and action roadmaps.

* * *

Chapter Nine

Process & Technology

Michael did not often visit Lee in what he came to think of as his lair. The IT floor was far quieter than any of the others and what snatches of conversation Michael did hear were incomprehensible to him. He didn't speak geek. His view was that all the IT guys really did was run the cables from his team's terminals to wherever it was the wires needed to go. His daughter had set up their WiFi network at home, and she was forever downloading this software or that app. He knew because she bought them on his account. If she could do all that without ever taking her eyes off Snapchat or popping even a single earbud from her ears temporarily to help her concentrate, what could all these people possibly be doing?

"Have you been in here before?" asked Lee, swiping his access card across the black box next to a frosted glass door. There was no sign on the door, Michael noticed.

"No," said Michael. "I didn't even know you had a walk-in wine refrigerator."

"This," said Lee, smiling, "is where the development team works. Nobody comes in here unless they have special access."

"I guess that makes you Q," said Michael, affecting what Lee marked down as one of the top three worst Sean Connery impressions he'd ever heard.

"Maybe, but you're no James Bond. I just want you to see something. Is it set up?" he asked a young man who was coming out of a breakout room. Michael noticed the man was wearing jeans—another reason he didn't like the IT floor.

"Good to go," the man said to Lee.

"Come in," said Lee, walking into the room the man had just left. There was a mobile phone on the table and Michael was on the verge of calling after the man in jeans when Lee picked it up and turned it on. "Sit next to me," he said to Michael.

Lee tapped an icon with Infinity's logo and typed in a password. The screen changed to an elegant design showing mostly numbers and a couple of charts, one of which was moving.

"That's a foreign exchange account," said Lee, anticipating Michael's question. "There's a lot of movement on the dollar and the value of my dollar account is updating in real time."

"So this is your portfolio?" asked Michael.

"It's a dummy portfolio we set up to test Infinity's next generation app," said Lee. "Have a look." He handed Michael the phone.

"I think I've found a glitch," said Michael, pointing to a graph. "There's no way iron ore prices have done that in the last twenty minutes. There's either a problem with the app or your dummy datasheet is missing a row."

"The portfolio is a dummy. The data feed is real and coming in live," said Lee. "Let's find out what's happening. Tap on that silhouette of a person in a headset."

"We're going to call the support team?" asked Michael. "I know what making a phone call is like, especially to a customer support team. I don't think I need a demo of that."

"Just press the button, Commander Bond," said Lee.

Michael did as he was told and the phone duly made a ringing noise. Suddenly, the screen was filled with the face of the man in jeans.

"Mr. Stockley, nice to see you. My name is Matt. How can I help you today?"

You could put on a tie, Michael thought to himself. Instead, he said, "Your minerals data are wrong."

"I can see the information showing on your app, Mr. Stockley. Is this the chart you're looking at?"

The full screen picture of Lee's role-playing tech guy went slightly opaque and an image of the iron ore price chart was superimposed on it. As Michael watched it, the line moved.

"As you can see, Mr. Stockley, there's some unusual velocity in the price today. The information is correct. There have been a couple of unexpected announcements from Australia today and the market has not taken it well. If you like, I can send copies of the announcements to your screen."

* * *

"So, what did you think?" asked Lee, as they walked out of the breakout room.

"That's quite something," said Michael.

"And no cables," said Lee, tilting his head and raising his eyebrows. Michael remembered there might have been a night in the bar he shared his view of IT with Lee.

"How did he have all that information about the market?"

Lee explained that call center staff were going to be given access to a new meta database that pulled information from multiple sources into one massive pool of information, and then sorted fact from fiction.

"Even with that sort of click-to-call technology built into the app, we know people will have read three things online and maybe even talked to a couple of other people before they call us," said Lee. "We need to be able see everything and know what's what."

"That's some serious technology," said Michael. "You can't tell me there aren't a lot of cables somewhere."

"It's not enough to be good at your core business anymore," said Lee. "Whatever business you're in, you have to be a master of technology too. If customers don't already expect technology, information, and access to be seamless, they soon will. And you wait till you see the reporting we're going to get. Obviously, our first-call resolution rate is going to go through the roof, but think of the other metrics. We'll be able to give people exactly what they want in terms of frequency of reporting and contact. Customers will basically be able to decide exactly how much they want to hear from us. Customers who want a lot of contact can have it. Customers who don't want to hear from us a lot don't have to. For your guys, imagine what it's going to do to their net promoter score when their customers can get this level of research, information, and support after they've bought a product. Come into my office and I'll show you what else we're planning."

"That really is excellent," said Michael. "The team will love it and it'll be good to have some good news to share with them.".

"Are you all right, Michael?" asked Lee.

Vision to Results Insights

If there is a business today that doesn't need to think about technology when it thinks about delivering on its strategy, we can't think of it. Today's customers expect more; they expect it quickly wherever they are; they expect it to be personalized, and they don't expect to pay more for it. That experience can't be delivered without technology.

Companies need to automate what they can. Automation in information is no different from automation in production: it makes things faster, it makes them cheaper, and it reduces errors. In Infinity's case, the CIO is looking at getting information to customers automatically and in real time. If the customers want less, they can adjust accordingly. However, the system doesn't rely on automation and technology at the expense of customer service, as Michael saw in his video conversation. What Lee and his team have managed to do in the prototype Michael saw is to put a human face on some sophisticated technology, none of which we imagined ourselves: everything Michael saw demonstrated is being used by our own clients today.

Having that level of access to their information and to a real person with up-to-the-minute information would, however, be entirely in line with Infinity's promise that working with them would be life changing.

When planning for technology to support a strategy, companies need to:

- Accept the new customer—almost any business in any industry will tell you their customers are not only more demanding but also better informed. That isn't going to change, so it's essential to be able to provide service at that level.

- Recognize the omnichannel world— customers have many devices and ways to make contact. Businesses need to make moving between them frictionless for the customer. They should have the same (exceptional) experience whether they visit you in person, come to your website, call your sales or customer support teams or use your latest app.

- Pick the metrics that matter—the growth in data means there's ever more that can be measured, but, as has always been the case, some metrics matter more than others. Infinity's new app, for instance, will generate all sorts of new information about customers (how often the log in, what they look at, for how long etc.). The organization needs to get advice on best practice and on the metrics that count.

* * *

Part Four

Sustain Momentum

Chapter Ten

Energy & Visibility

Usually the first to arrive on a Monday morning, Robert stopped in his tracks when he saw Michael, sitting at the desk next to his. Until recently, the space next to him had been a hot desk for salespeople coming in from Infinity's other offices. Now there were framed pictures of Michael's two children on top of the desk, along with the father-of-the-year coffee mug the children had bought him, which was sitting on top of the current edition of the Harvard Business Review. A wisp of steam hovered above the nearly-full mug.

"Morning," said Michael, looking up briefly from his keyboard and nodding at Robert.

"Morning," said Robert, putting his shoulder bag on the floor and pulling out his laptop. "Michael?"

"Yes?" said Michael, swiveling the chair in his direction.

"I can't help noticing that you're sitting here and not in your office."

"What office?" said Michael.

"The nice one in the corner. The one with the view down the river. You know, my office in about five years."

"I'm afraid your next office just became our new meeting room," said Michael. "I've decided to come out where the action is or—in your case—where the action isn't."

"So I've lost my future office and gained a comedy desk mate?"

"I can't expect you to be out here getting on with it while I'm tucked away behind glass, like a museum exhibit."

"Do you know, when I came in and saw someone at that desk I was expecting it to be someone else," said Robert, his tone becoming more serious.

"I can imagine who," said Michael grimly.

*　*　*

A jogger turned the corner as Scott got out of the car to give it a quick once over with a cloth before the morning run into the city.

"Morning," said the jogger from behind him, a little out of breath.

Scott recognized the voice immediately. He spun round amazed to see Alex Dalton in a black tracksuit with a towel round his neck.

"I slightly underestimated how long that was going to take me," said Alex, his breath coming out in a light fog.

"Are you okay if I take half an hour to shower and get dressed?"

"No problem, Mr. Dalton," said Scott, noticing the brand new trainers on his client's feet and the high tech shirt and jacket he was wearing.

*   *   *

Twenty minutes later, Alex was in the back seat looking more familiar in an immaculately tailored suit, with not a hair out of place. The only reminder of their earlier encounter was the Tritan water bottle Alex was holding. Scott couldn't help glancing in the mirror every time Alex took a drink. The silicone mouthpiece was opaque but it looked like what was flowing through it was emerald green.

"My wife makes a mean green smoothie," said Alex, when he noticed Scott's interest. "When I say 'mean' I should probably say 'evil,' but she swears it's good for me and she's not trying to kill me."

"What's in it?" asked Scott.

"I've decided not to ask," said Alex. "I think it's better I don't know, but as you might have inferred from our encounter on the path this morning, I've decided it's time for a change. Work had been sucking the life out of me for so long it had started to feel normal to get out of bed feeling that way. I'd forgotten what it was like to have energy, a bit of bounce."

"And the jogging and the smoothies are helping?" asked Scott.

"They certainly help me look forward to lunch," said Alex.

They both laughed as the car glided through the early morning traffic.

*   *   *

In short order, Michael had had a version of the same conversation with every member of the team as they arrived. By 8:30, everyone was at their desks. Michael pushed back his chair and stood up.

"All right, everyone, if you could gather round," he said.

"Is it someone's birthday?" asked Rachel, leaning over and whispering to Robert.

"Don't ask me," said Robert. "I've no idea what's going on."

"No, it isn't anyone's birthday," said Michael, turning to look in their direction. "That's right, I hear really well when I'm not behind glass." He grinned at Rachel before turning back to the sales team, now on their feet and standing around him. Behind him, the team's A3 progress chart showed a zero for the first time in the box for sales of Infinity's officially discontinued products.

"Unaccustomed as I am to being so close to you all, I figure I might as well make the most of it. This is how we're going to start every day."

"You're not going to have us touching our toes are you?" Jeremy called from the back.

"When was the last time you even saw you toes?" Robert shot back, to good-natured laughter from the group.

"Thank you, children," Michael continued. "There will be no touching in these huddles. What there will be is a quick run around the group, with each of you telling the rest of us what you're working on and whether you've learned anything interesting since the last time."

"'Interesting'?" said Matt. "That's a bit unfair on Darren, isn't it?" More laughter.

"I'll start us off with an example," said Michael. "Yesterday, I had a call from one of our oldest clients to tell me how impressed recently he'd been by Jeremy. He said he hadn't had a salesman do so much listening and so little talking in the whole time he'd been in this business. So, well done, Jeremy."

Jeremy blushed, and a couple of those standing next to him patted him on the back.

"In honor of Jeremy's achievements, I would like to present him with this award."

Michael walked over to Jeremy, while fishing in the pocket of his jacket. He pulled out a novelty trophy the height of his thumb and passed the miniature cup to Jeremy, shaking his hand with mock seriousness.

"Speech," shouted Rachel.

"Words could not adequately describe how honored I am to have been recognized in this way," said Jeremy, pulling his hand into his stomach and taking a low theatrical bow.

"I thought you didn't want to touch your toes this morning," said Robert.

"The next time one of you does something spectacular, the trophy will pass to you, but for now, Jeremy, it's all yours to enjoy," said Michael.

Jeremy grinned at the laughter and the light smattering of applause from his colleagues.

"More seriously, I'm sitting out here now because this is a team effort, and I know it helps when the leader actually knows what's going on. Me being out here and these huddles in the morning are going to help with that. The other thing they're going to do is keep me honest. From now on, when you ask me for a decision, we're going to agree when I'll come back to you. If I haven't kept up my end of the deal, you get to call me on it here, and if you're right, I owe the whole group a coffee. Fair?"

The group made it clear that they did indeed think it was fair. Michael caught a movement in the corner of his eye and turned to see Alex leaning on a wall to the left of the group. It looked as if he might have been there for a while.

The two men's eyes met. Michael gave a slight nod and Alex returned the greeting with a big smile on his face as he turned and walked back to his office. On his way, he noticed Kathryn and her team were in a meeting room. Through the glass, he could see Piet drawing what looked like a mind map on the whiteboard. There was no doubt about it; there was vibrancy about the place that reminded him of the company's first years.

* * *

It seemed a long time since Heather had first speculated there might be a slight spring in Alex's step on the day he called them together to talk about Infinity's lack of vision. These days, he seemed to positively exude vitality.

It is, she thought, as she brought her coffee up to her lips, *enviable.* She flipped open the Louis Vuitton cover and glanced down at the Infinity management app on her phone. It had been Lee's idea to give all of them access to the latest information on various metrics. It was similar in thinking to the portfolio management app Michael had seen demonstrated in the IT lab, which was now only weeks from launch. When you can see the information, Lee had reminded them, you're more likely to act on it.

Although Heather couldn't press a button to a launch a video call with a colleague, she was pleased to see the charts showing net promoter score was rising almost across the board. Clicking on the chart for a detailed view of her own team, she was particularly pleased to see that Pratik's score was the most improved of all of them. She looked up, caught Pratik's eye, and smiled.

Pratik and Andrea were sitting on the other side of the polished wood table in the boardroom. Kathryn was talking to Andrea about the work she had been doing with Samira on honing the employee value proposition. It had been Alex's idea that whenever possible they should invite people outside the executive team to their meetings.

Alex had suggested it would give them another perspective, but more importantly, it would show the rest of the company that the executive team was going through the same change process, using the same tools and being held to the same vision as everyone else.

"Good morning again, everyone. Shall we get started?" said Alex, from the head of the long table.

Vision to Results Insights

Energy and visibility are different things, of course, but they're so closely linked to each other that they form a single VTR driver of strategy execution. When leaders lack energy, confidence, and excitement in their companies, they're likely to be absent, to hide in their offices, and be seen less often. Other people in the organization see that and it is contagious. When leaders check out, the entire organization loses momentum. Lack of visibility is so easily interpreted as a lack of energy that leaders who are full of energy but out of sight for other reasons need to make a special effort to find time to be seen.

Energy is not just an abstract concept that applies to whether an organization feels like it has focus. Individual health is key to business success, as Alex is rediscovering by starting to take better care of himself. Being in better health translates to more energy, better productivity, and greater happiness. Spending all your time at your desk and not looking out for your wellbeing—and that of your employees—will not make you a better leader. The green smoothie is optional, but taking care of yourself is not.

When Alex walks the floor in the morning and sees Michael's first huddle and the communications team having an early meeting, he is tapped into the pulse of the organization. Rather than taking the elevator up to a special floor and relying on filtered reports, he can see for himself that the organization is still excited about its vision and direction. Leaders need to check in frequently with the greater organization or they will eventually find themselves surprised by something they should have seen coming.

Visibility relates to the visibility of leaders and not just because that translates to energy. As Michael demonstrates, it also translates to action. The longer it takes to get hold of a decision maker, the longer it takes to get things done.

It also relates to progress reports. As we've seen repeatedly in the Infinity story, things get done when people have clarity about where they are, where they're going, and what they need to do to get there. In the Infinity office, the sales team has chosen to measure how many legacy products they sell. The monthly tally is on the wall in front of everyone. Lee has given the executive team an app so they can see up-to-date information about all the organization's key metrics.

We include an element of transparency in the question of visibility as well. Many of the things discussed at the executive level don't have to be confidential. The more secretive you're seen to be, the more people will fill in the gaps by making up stories to explain what they think they're not being told. By opening up his meetings to people from across the organization, Alex is showing, rather than just telling, Infinity that they are all on the same path.

When thinking about the Energy and Visibility aspect of the VTR framework, leaders should:

- Consider the basic question of health—you can't mandate fitness but you can certainly encourage it with incentives, group activities and by modeling it yourself.
- Be visible—it's as simple as it sounds. How many people have you made yourself available to this week? Walking the floor is an obvious way to see and be seen. If people are spread out, there are phone calls, video conferences and other ways to check in. You

know whether you're visible to your team or not. The trick is to keep asking yourself whether you are.

- Check other people's energy levels—be open with people, ask questions, check that they are excited about what's happening. If they aren't, find out why not. One idea would be to spend a day a month without opinions of your own—make the most possible room for other people to tell you what they think should happen.

- Be as transparent as possible—some things are confidential, many things aren't. Don't make secrets out of things that don't need to be. Show people that you really are all part of one big team.

*　*　*

Chapter Eleven

Accountability

"Good, good," said Alex.

Kathryn had just finished presenting the work her team and Heather's had been doing together.

"It seems we're on track with incorporating the vision into the employee value proposition," said Alex. "It certainly looks like our gut feeling was right. People are looking for a new kind of place to work. And, even more importantly, the focus groups and the market are telling us there's definitely room for a new kind of approach."

"There is one more thing we'd like to do," said Heather. "We're having a bit of trouble getting the right people in IT to help us get some of this content on the web. Lee, if you could get someone to work with Samira and Karen, that would be a big help."

"That's no problem," said Lee.

"The website is obviously a big part of getting this message out there," said Alex. "Lee, you need to get involved in this. We can't be taking an individual view of these projects. Let's go through the projects list again and see where we should be helping each other. And we shouldn't be waiting to be asked."

After they had discussed the list and made some commitments about joint actions, Alex moved to the next item on the agenda: sales.

"Michael," he said, pressing his fingertips together, "my understanding is that our existing customers haven't been getting the full picture about where Infinity is going, and what that means for them. Would you agree?"

"It is," said Michael, shifting in his seat. His voice was strained. "Admittedly, there's no doubt some of the team are better at positioning the change than others. Customers aren't always getting an enthusiastic presentation of the new Infinity, and the sales team isn't listening to customers as well as they should. It's something Heather has agreed her team will work on in the sales academy. There will be an even stronger focus on bringing everyone we can up to the new standard or perhaps bringing in new people."

"So it's Heather's responsibility?"

"That's not what I'm saying," said Michael, his voice taking on a staccato quality. "Heather is helping me to work out what kind of development is needed to get the team doing what we need."

"That's aptly put," said Alex, looking the management app on the screen in front of him, "because they're definitely not doing what we need now. According to this, almost half of what we sold in the last month were products we'd agreed we were not going to be selling anymore. Whose responsibility is that?"

"I think," said Michael, with obvious effort to compose himself, "you and I have a couple of things to work through."

An uncomfortable silence fell over the room.

* * *

Alex and Michael had no trouble finding a table in the bar. It was only 4 pm, too early for most of the bar's regular clientele to be even thinking about their day coming to an end. They chose a raised booth in the back of the room and ordered two beers. The two men exchanged small talk until the waitress brought back the bottles.

"What's going on, Michael?" asked Alex, after the two men had taken their first drinks.

"It's like I said in the meeting this morning. Some of the team needs more training, and some probably need to be somewhere else."

"Look, I didn't want to have this conversation in front of the whole team because what you're saying isn't really good enough. Is it?"

"Alex, I didn't bring this team over with me when I came to Infinity. They're my team now, sure. But

I didn't pick them. I inherited them, and they need some work. That's what I'm doing. That's what the academy is for."

"Let's call a spade a spade. This isn't about the quality of the sales team," said Alex. "It's about the quality of the leadership."

"You're telling me," replied Michael, drawing on his beer. "I've got the sales managers going out with the sales people. I thought we'd get better results that way, but they're no better. The managers are just as set in their ways as their people. We need to give the whole team a push, to change their thinking, and their approach."

Alex rested his elbows on the table between them and leaned forward, his fingers interlocked. He looked directly into Michael's eyes. "I'm not talking about the leadership in the middle, Michael. I'm talking about you."

"You think this is my fault?" said Michael, putting his beer down heavily. "I've got what's essentially everyone else's team and a radical rethink of the way we're doing thing, but I'm supposed to have the whole machine oiled and running faultlessly in a matter of weeks?"

"You're right, Michael, it was a big ask. That's why—"

"Yes, it was, Alex," said Michael cutting him off. "It was a big ask. And I've been doing everything possible to make it happen. We took responsibility as a team for making this change, and I've owned my part of it. I've got some people issues and I'm working on them."

"This morning, I got the impression you had Heather working on them for you."

"That's not fair," said Michael, sitting up straight on his stool. "I said she was helping me."

"And that's good," said Alex. "But you should have known already that your team was going to find this adjustment as hard as they have. You've got Heather helping you assess capabilities that I think you should have known about already."

"There's a possibility," said Michael, looking towards the corner of the room, "that I haven't worked as closely with the sales managers as I should have been."

"Why do you think you haven't?"

"I was perhaps too guided by the numbers," said Michael. "They were making their targets, but I should have spent more time looking at how they were making those numbers. I would have seen they weren't tuned in enough to the customers for it to have been sustainable."

"All right. But I think there's a bigger problem," said Alex.

"I think you're right," said Michael.

"And what do you think it is?"

"It's you," said Michael.

* * *

Michael explained to Alex that he had felt consistently undermined since Infinity had set out its new strategy.

"Sales is crucial to every business, so I'm used to a certain amount of backstopping, but not to this level," said Michael. "You started coming to sales meetings, which was great. But were you at as many HR team meetings? Were you at that many of Lee's meetings in IT? Every time I called a client, it would turn out you'd been on the phone an hour before. You went on sales calls with my team."

"We agreed that leadership would be more visible," said Alex. "We needed to show people, as well as tell them, that this was a significant change, that it had all our attention."

"There's a difference between showing people that a project has the CEO's full attention and suggesting that he doesn't have confidence in his team." Michael realized he had raised his voice and sat back in the booth. "You wanted an open exchange of views. That's my view."

"Sales were down," said Alex. "I'm the CEO. The performance of this company is, ultimately, my responsibility."

"Of course sales were down," said Michael. "We were radically changing what we sold and who we sold it to. Our whole model now is actually to not sell things to some people, if the product doesn't fit the customer. We anticipated that."

"It wasn't my intention to undermine you," said Alex, said after a moment.

"It doesn't matter what your intention was," said Michael, taking a drink. "It matters what people saw and what they thought it meant."

Alex put his hand across his chin. He had expected confrontation and thought it was necessary to clear the air. He hadn't, if he were honest, expected that there would be another point of view to his own. The two men sat in silence for a short while.

Alex was the one to break the silence. "Regardless of the sales team's ability to listen to customers or whether they even believe in the way Infinity is going, you told them that we were taking products off the market. Half your team was responsible for deciding which those products should be. The other half was working on new products. The result is that no one in the team was in any doubt that things were changing. Regardless of whether they were for it or against it, they knew the change was happening."

"That's true," said Michael, "but I don't get what you're saying."

"They knew what was scheduled to be withdrawn. They knew what we were focusing on selling. You told them not to sell particular products but they carried on selling them anyway, not a little but a lot. Almost half of what they sold was on the list of products to be discontinued."

"It takes time to put the brakes on something like this."

"Michael, this came from the top. You are the head of sales. They knew you'd told them to stop selling these things, and they carried on anyway."

"Like I just told you, it didn't feel like I was the 'top'," said Michael.

"I take your point. I got too involved," said Alex. "But you have to admit that I never said anything to contradict you. Our roles might have gotten confused in some people's minds but the message never did."

"That's true," said Michael.

"So, the fact is that something got disconnected here and it has to get reconnected. They need a change in leadership."

"You're firing me?" said Michael, incredulously.

"No, I'm not, because I think some of the blame for this lies with me. My view was that if you managed to get this disconnected from your team without my noticing it, then I let you down, too. I see now that it was even more than that. Not only did I not notice, but I'm also partly responsible for that disconnection. But, I am aware of it now. I will take a step back to make sure no one is confused about where their direction is coming from, but your leadership has to change because the numbers are clear. I don't think, even when you take my intervention out of the equation, that the way you're running that team is working. And you have to work out how you're going to get things on track," said Alex, lifting his bottle to his lips. "Fast."

Vision to Results Insights

Alex's experiences in this chapter illustrate that real life is messier than can ever be captured by a model on paper. It would be convenient if we could work through each step of the model and move onto the next only once we had everything perfect, never looking back. In real life, there is overlap and sometimes it's necessary to go back to a step in order to move forward.

In the Enable & Execute stage of VTR, Infinity's teams laid out their action roadmaps detailing which actions had priority. It's common for leaders to get too involved in the execution of those roadmaps. They are even more likely to dive in when something starts to appear slightly adrift. By getting overly immersed in the detail, they lose sight of the big picture.

In Infinity's case, sales numbers dipped as the organization executed on its new strategy. Alex's response was to get overly involved in the workings of the sales team. Of course crises occur and events crop up unexpectedly, but leaders need to keep an eye on the long term and the bigger picture. As Michael points out to Alex, a short-term reduction in sales was anticipated.

Infinity and its executive team are on the right track, however. Leaders are being held to account, not only for their own actions but jointly for the performance of the whole organization. Alex has made it clear that he's not interested in an approach where a senior leader is considered to be doing okay just because their area is in good shape. Collective accountability is crucial to high performance, but equally, leaders need to be able and willing to ask for help when they need it.

Alex himself has also been held to account by a member of his team. Michael should have done it sooner, but he has now spoken up and caused Alex to reflect on his part in the problems faced by the sales team. The next step for Infinity might be to institute a more formal feedback process. If Alex had been asking his team for feedback, he probably would have found out sooner the effect of his over-involvement in the day-to-day running of the sales team.

Central to effectively running an accountable organization:

- People should be encouraged to ask for help when they need it (and be held to account if things go wrong because they didn't ask for help when they should have);
- Collective accountability should be demonstrated at the highest levels;
- Embedding a culture of authentic feedback is essential to encourage people to speak freely. Helping people have these critical conversations is key;
- Clear performance goals and objectives should be established, behavior monitored, and feedback provided, and you should make sure you tap into the strengths and talents of your people.

*　*　*

Chapter Twelve

Continuous Improvement

Heather threw back her head and laughed, slapping Michael on the shoulder.

"What's the joke?" asked Kathryn, turning her attention from Lee and leaning across the table.

"Oh, you wouldn't get it, Kathryn. You'd have to know something about sales," said Michael.

"You just wait," said Lee, grinning. "It won't be long before the sales team is just an algorithm generated in IT."

"I know, I know," said Michael. "One day, we'll all be just the pets of our geek rulers from IT, so for now we'd better eat, drink, and be merry. To Infinity Investments." He raised his wine glass and the three of them clinked their glasses. "And beyond," he added.

Heather took a drink from her glass and shared a smile with Kathryn. Not long ago, she would have dreaded an evening like this, another attempt by Alex to forge a bond between a dysfunctional team. Tonight, she was having a blast. A private dining room, a chef at the height of his reputation, and a team that ranked among the best she'd ever worked with. The wine wasn't bad either. Her moment of reflection was interrupted by the chiming of a wine glass from the end of the table. Alex stood up with his glass in his hand.

"As the toasts have already begun, it seems like a good time to throw in my own," he said. "This has been an extraordinary year and it has been my privilege to work with all of you on what has been—"

"Life changing!" heckled Michael, to laughter.

"Exactly," said Alex. "We have gone from not being sure who we were to being able to claim some of the happiest clients in the industry. That has come, as we hoped and as Michael will be the first to tell you, with some of the healthiest sales numbers in the industry, too. We are, in fact, leading in more than one of our biggest markets. Thank you, Michael, for taking charge of what needed to be done in the sales team in what were, I know, not always the easiest circumstances." He looked at Michael and raised his glass. "Along the way, we have reminded ourselves that if you let yourself stand still in business, you will soon be going backwards. But, a year ago, we set a direction, we headed out towards it, and we brought the entire company with us. I couldn't then have imagined how far we would come in such a short time. And we have, of course, picked up some travelers to join us on that journey. We welcomed Aaron to the team."

He raised his glass in the direction of the recently appointed CXO. "Having someone to remind us constantly that the customer is the center of this company is another important step. There will many more of those steps this year, but thanks to everything you and your teams have done, we can take those steps faster and with even more enthusiasm. Speaking of which, as you know, we're here tonight because tomorrow is a year to the day that we set our vision of life-changing experiences. And tomorrow we gather in the boardroom to talk about where we go from here. We have won, we have learned from what we've done, and we will continue to change. I can't wait to hear what plans you have for that. To what's next!" He raised his glass in the air.

"What's next!" the team said in unison, raising their own glasses happily.

Vision to Results Insights

Vision to Results is about a win-learn-win view of the world. At every stage in the framework, lessons will be learned and they will come from victories as much as failures. Gold medalists don't stop reviewing their tapes and looking for what they could do better next time. Infinity has pulled itself back to the top of its game, but it would quickly start going backwards again if it were to rest there.

VTR is a loop, and continuous reflection and improvement is essential. An organization needs to measure itself constantly. The best plans are meaningless if their implementation is not measured.

Constant attention is needed to make sure the organization is working to improve itself in the areas of greatest importance. Common areas of high priority include:

- Getting a better understanding of customers;
- Inspiring mindset change and high levels of engagement;

- Creating a competitive differentiator through technology and operational process; and
- Predicting and working out how to adapt to an increasingly competitive environment.

That might be sound exhausting, but an organization that has aligned itself to this framework will be full of energy and optimism about what needs to be done. The idea of further change will be invigorating, not draining.

And, a loop wins every time over a downward spiral.

With things looking up for Infinity, it will be time for the organization to think about reinvesting the operational savings or the increase in profits that the change in direction and focus have delivered. Tomorrow, its leaders will talk about what those investments might be. We would imagine technology would be high on the agenda, seeking solutions aimed at opening new markets or bringing in more customers. They should talk about what technology might be able to do to retain existing customers and offer them new products and services. Perhaps Kathryn in the communications team will be looking for a solution that gives the organization more predictive insights into customers.

Alex and his team have obviously changed the culture of Infinity Investments and that is reflected in the results the organization has achieved and in their own energized team dynamic. There is no doubt, however, that next year will be one of massive change. And, so will the next. That is what will make Infinity a great organization to work for into the future.

* * *

Epilogue

The black town car was making good speed through the light late-night traffic.

"If you don't mind me saying, Mr. Dalton, you've been looking lighter for quite a while now," said the driver.

"I'm not sure that's going to last after this evening, Scott. Not after that meal."

"That's not the sort of weight I'm taking about, Mr. Dalton, and I think you know it."

"You're right, Scott. Infinity's a very different place from this time last year. It feels like we're playing in another league."

"So I've read," said Scott, tilting his head in the direction of the iPad on the passenger seat next to him. The business section of that day's paper had carried a half-page feature on the remarkable turnaround in Infinity's fortunes. Infinity was being held up as an example to an industry in need of radical change. "It looks like you worked out where you were going, even without a GPS for business."

ALEX
DALTON,
C.E.O

SCOTT
BOYLAN,
HIS DRIVER

HEATHER
WONG
Head of H.R.

MICHAEL
STOCKLEY
Sales Director

KATHRYN
CHIVERS
Communications
Director

LEE
WASHINGTON
C.I.O

JULIA
Receptionist

KIRSTY
Alex's P.A

ALI
Call Centre
Employee

THE SALES TEAM

JEREMY   ROBERT   RACHEL   MATT & DARREN

THE H.R TEAM

PRATIK   VERONIQUE   KAREN   ANDREA
deputy head

THE COMMS TEAM

I.T

PIET   SAMIRA   TIM

PLUS...

DAVID THE ARTIST

"Actually, you know what, Scott?" said Alex. "I think we might just have found one."

*   *   *

The Vision to Results Framework

Applying the art of leadership and delivering the results you desire from the vision you set.

Ask 100 chief executives for the key to effective leadership in business and a high proportion will answer: "The ability to set a clear vision, translate that into a consistent strategy, and deliver results."

So, why do so many leaders fail by the one yardstick that really matters: results? Why are so many good strategies so poorly executed? What makes so many talented and intelligent leaders, who passionately believe in the course they are setting, unable to mobilize their workforce effectively and get their teams to buy into the plan?

It's not as if leaders don't know what to do. They know they're expected to inspire their troops and bring them into the battle, confident of victory. But how do they do that? Inspiring and motivating people are one of the hardest tasks in life. Business leaders are constantly bombarded with peers telling them what they should be doing. They are subjected to feedback reports, behavioral 360s, staff engagement surveys, and advice from the board. Yet, the role of the leader is so complex with respect to the successful delivery of strategy that it needs to be demystified, and reinforced with practical step-by-step reminders so none are overlooked, bypassed, or assumed.

TRUTH #1: Extraordinary leadership requires a relentless focus on what is most important, balanced with an ability to motivate and understand people.

In 2005, the Human Resources director of a large organization rang one of our Directors, desperately seeking some advice over coffee. The chief executive was determined to turn his company into a more accountable organization. When our Director asked why the workforce wasn't already considered sufficiently accountable, his client replied: "Because they never do what we ask them to do!"

Our Director recognized that the problem lay not with the workforce alone, but to a large degree with the leader. Was the leader concentrating his energies sufficiently on ALL of the elements of leadership required to guarantee the success?

The solution was the development of a step-by-step framework designed specifically to make the leader aware of the leadership responsibilities and activities required for success. Often, when a strategy is not executed successfully, the leader blames the workforce; the lack of results must mean individual members of the team haven't been working hard enough or have only half-heartedly grasped the strategy. But who is ultimately responsible for the failed execution? The Leader.

When our Director first presented the Vision to Results (VTR) framework, with its 12 key topics, on a single page to the CEO and his senior executives, something magical happened. The CEO realized that if the strategy was ever going to work, it wasn't only his team that would need to do things differently in the future, but that he would have to change his focus too.

TRUTH #2: Most strategies fail NOT because of the strength of the strategy itself but rather because the leader rushed too quickly from formulating the strategy to focusing on its implementation.

Too little time and thought are put into the vital intermediate stages.

- WHY is the strategy so important for the company?
- WHAT are the consequences of it not being executed properly, both for the organization and the individual?

- WHAT mechanisms can be put in place to ensure individual team members know exactly what their personal responsibilities are for implementing the strategy?
- HOW will their performance be monitored?
- WHAT will be the consequences if they fail to deliver?
- HOW can we measure and celebrate success along the journey?

Leaders often assume that because they've addressed a team meeting, held an in-depth briefing for senior executives, conducted an all-staff meeting, or explained the plan in an email, that the job of selling the strategy to the workforce has been done.

TRUTH #3: Humans need to have both goal and role clarity connected to the strategy if a leader is to have any chance of gaining their energy and focus.

How many times do people nod enthusiastically at the end of a meeting when asked if they understand a new strategy and how it will require a substantial change in the way they work—only to revert to their old work practices at the first sign of difficulty? The key to success is ALIGNMENT—in both thought and action. Ultimately, it is the leader's responsibility to insist that messages are cascaded accurately and appropriately down to each level involved in implementing the strategy. Each person on the team must be aware of how the strategy translates into specific actions for them. And crucially, how the strategy will benefit them individually. Never underestimate the driving power of: "What's in it for me?"

TRUTH #4: Team performance is often a direct reflection of the leader's ability to inspire and engage.

Since 2009, we have been gathering data from the frontline; providing invaluable evidence of how people perceive vital issues in their businesses. One of the key findings in our most recent Global Mindset Index—compiled from approximately 5,000 clients representing 40 companies around the world—was that 43 percent of respondents felt their leaders had failed to create a motivational environment. That's a damning statistic. Almost half felt their leaders had not succeeding in motivating them.

Further research shows that leaders consistently mislead themselves, assuming they have communicated their intentions to their staff and that the whole organization is working effectively and whole-heartedly for the same objective. Our surveys reveal the sad truth. Where there should be clarity, there is confusion. Where there should be commitment, there is disillusionment. So where do we go from here?

The Vision to Results Framework

Vision to Results (VTR) is a framework consisting of 12 drivers that clearly outline the baseline leadership activities we believe are essential to position the leader, team and/or organization for execution success.

Vision to Results (VTR) deconstructs the entire complex process—from setting a vision to delivering the ultimate result required—in one easily-understood framework that ensures both the rational and the emotional aspects of a plan are properly addressed, in the correct order, with sufficient weight and balance.

The beauty of VTR lies in its simplicity. It can be used by any leader of any organization, no matter how big or small, to lead a team from the development of a strategy to its successful delivery. What it is NOT is a "silver bullet," a "panacea," or "the new big thing." Ultimately, leading any organization or team is hard work. Those leaders who have a clear vision, a logical strategy, understand what they want to achieve, are disciplined in executing the strategy while holding their teams and themselves to account, are far more likely to deliver the results. VTR ensures this happens by addressing both the Rational and Emotional criteria necessary for successful execution.

Understandably, most leaders tend to concentrate on the RATIONAL elements of implementing a strategy because they can be "ticked off," one by one, and assigned to the "mission accomplished" file.

- Does the vision clearly set out where we want to go? Does it include some stretch?
- Is the strategy grounded in reality? Are sufficient resources allocated at each level of the plan?
- Have we created a comprehensive accountability culture? Do we have the right level of competence at each grade to deliver on the plan?

But effective leadership execution requires far more than intellectual logic. Busy leaders intent on rolling out their master plan often fail to address the equally important EMOTIONAL criteria that must be fulfilled if a plan is to be successful. One of the most common failings we see is leaders who fail to realize that the people side of their job is NEVER complete. Motivation is not a box that can be ticked off. Just because someone has been told what the new strategy is and appears confident and engaged doesn't mean he will remain that way.

The Twelve Drivers of Strategy Execution

How it works

There are four stages in the VTR framework. Two are "rational" (Set Direction and Enable & Execute).

Rational	**SET DIRECTION**	VISION
		STRATEGY
		ASSESSMENT
Emotional	**ENGAGE & EXCITE**	BELIEVABILITY
		DESIRABILITY
		COMMUNICATION
Rational	**ENABLE & EXECUTE**	ACTION ROADMAP
		CAPABILITY DEVELOPMENT
		PROCESS & TECHNOLOGY
Emotional	**SUSTAIN MOMENTUM**	ENERGY & VISIBILITY
		ACCOUNTABILITY
		CONTINUOUS IMPROVEMENT

Create Context

Drive Performance

Two are "emotional" (Engage & Excite and Sustain Momentum). Six of the elements lie in the "Create Context" section above the dotted line, indicating they are about setting the goal (direction of the company/new project/product launch) and engaging the people/ resources to make it happen. The six elements in the "Drive Performance" section below the dotted line are concerned with getting the vision done and producing results. The Rational elements are targets that can be achieved and completed. The Emotional elements require constant attention and reinforcement.

The first six elements create the context for the performance—including the rewards for getting it right and the consequences for not following through.

Set Direction

Most leaders underestimate the importance and time needed to set up a really solid platform for their team's performance in delivering the leader's goals.

Driver: Vision

We've all been in those meetings when someone mentions vision and we witness a collective roll of the eyes. Many organizations don't even bother with a formal vision, tending to think of it as something woolly and intangible. But the vision doesn't have to be overly grandiose or changing the way the world thinks. It should be based on relevant conditions the organization faces and truly tap into aspirational performance. Take a global medical services client who knew the culture and performance they desired but struggled to articulate it in multiple locations and regions. We helped sculpt a vision that was compelling, values based, and included stretch. The most required quality is for the leader to focus on CLARITY. What is he or she trying to achieve? Why? Can it be clearly communicated? Will it inspire those who ultimately have to deliver it?

Driver: Strategy

Leaders are usually comfortable with establishing where they believe the organization should go. What they struggle with is the question: how to get there? Take the group of young computer entrepreneurs who came to us with an audacious vision. They wanted to sell their company once it had reached a market capitalization of US$500 million, and retire. We facilitated their thinking to help them devise a strategy to do just that. The truth is: most leaders are good at strategy. But if the strategy doesn't deliver the desired results, it's a failure. So the leader needs to ask: What will I do to make sure my plans are understood and acted upon? Is my strategy clear, consistent, and relevant to the people expected to implement it?

Driver: Assessment

Is the strategy realistic? Is it accepted as realistic? And should it be? Consider the Columbus Crew scenario. When Columbus set sail in 1492 from Palos de la Frontera with his flotilla of three ships, he was convinced the Earth was round. Were his crew equally committed? Like any sensible workforce, they probably had their doubts. But they had enough confidence in their commander, his leadership skills and—crucially—their reward package, to give it their best shot. Reality testing is becoming increasingly important. In the wake of the Global Financial Crisis, our leading clients now insist that new launches, products, or strategies are closely examined for flaws or false assumptions by their would-be customers before any rollout takes place. But that's not exactly a new discovery. Columbus went through many years (and several monarchs—Portugal, Genoa, Venice) before he was able to convince the Spanish throne that his venture was realistic.

Engage & Excite

For almost a decade, we have utilized the Vision to Results (VTR) framework in numerous executive scenarios. Time and time again, this crucial buy-in stage is missed or downplayed. We've found when facilitating groups that the more senior the executives, the more likely they are to confirm that they personally believe in the business's vision and strategy. (Of course they do. They were the ones who wrote it!) What is far more revealing is their answer to the follow-up question about desirability: Are you willing to change your own habitual behavior in order to get a different result? Suddenly, the room goes quiet. Though the need to engage and excite staff is common sense, it is simply not common practice.

Driver: Believability

People need to believe that a strategy will work and that they will personally benefit before they will alter the way they operate. Unless the senior leadership team not only buys into the delivery of the strategy but is also able to cascade its merits and importance down through each subsequent level of the organization, the results can never be anything more than unexceptional. Leaders, therefore, must focus time and energy on acquiring the skills of persuasion, explanation, communication, and reiteration. No one ever willingly followed a leader in whom they did not believe. And whatever the leader can do to make the journey seem less daunting for those about to embark on it, the better.

For example, we sometimes quote research conducted in the United States around a loyalty program at a car wash. The incentive was easy to understand: Every eight car washes the customer paid for entitled them to a free car wash. The sample group was split into two. One was given a loyalty card with the obvious nine spaces—for eight paid services and a bonus ninth car wash for free. The other group was given a loyalty card with ten spaces, with the first space already filled in. Both groups had the same challenge—pay for eight, get the ninth free. But the second group, which already had its card started, achieved the end result (the free car wash) 40 percent quicker than the first group.

Humans are more likely to finish what they have already started rather than start afresh. If the leader can show how far the team has already traveled on the road to the ultimate destination, the more believable that destination will appear to those on the trek.

Driver: Desirability

Even if someone believes a strategy is good for the organization, why would they bother enforcing it if it just meant more work for no more pay? Many leaders fail to understand that just because they are paying their sales team a good salary package, it doesn't mean those same people will agree—or more importantly, deliver the latest addition to their workload. It helps if the company has a bonus scheme in place to reward people who help deliver the strategy. But desirability is about more than material benefits. For the team to have the desire to make the project a success, it needs to understand:

- WHY the leader has initiated the strategy.
- WHAT it means for them individually.
- WHAT are the implications and consequences for the individual if the desired outcome isn't delivered.

Driver: Communication

In the context of strategy execution, communications is a core competency that, when properly executed, connects every member of an organization to a common set of strategies, goals, and actions. Unless these components are effectively shared by leaders and understood by stakeholders, results are jeopardized and budgets incur unnecessary risk.

Despite this risk, many organizations admit that they are currently not placing adequate importance on effectively communicating the vision, strategy, or change narrative—especially when explaining the business benefits of strategic initiatives to people at all levels of the organization. People need to understand WHY the strategy is important, WHAT it means to them on a daily basis, and HOW they are going to win in the customer's mind.

Many leaders simply rely on traditional communication to translate and cascade their vision and strategy for the organization, and then they wonder why, time and time again, the wider team asks for more detail. Engaging a wider range of stakeholders, including the executive leadership, in sharing the vision and strategy accelerates the cascade and raises the chance that the messaging will be authentic and understood.

Enable & Execute

Unless the leader's targets and workforce are aligned, success is highly unlikely. Yet, that alignment rarely happens well. The leader's job is to address the next three drivers and make sure that each person involved in the delivery is aware of their responsibilities, is clear on his specific role, has the skills and competencies required to deliver, and has considered technology and operational improvements to accelerate the desired results.

Driver: Action Roadmap

Any project/initiative/policy change will have potential blockages or massive consequences if the overall strategy isn't realized. The leader's job is to assign what needs to be done: By when? By what route? By whom? Then the leader needs to put in place a system to make sure deadlines are met, tasks completed, and potential blockages in the pipeline cleared before they appear. Simultaneously, the leader has to create their prioritized leadership activities to ensure the project stays on track. We help our client create what we refer to as a Plan on a Page (POAP).

Driver: Capability Development

Are the correct people in the correct key positions to deliver the desired results? Just because they were right for the last project, do they still have the correct knowledge, skills, processes, and mindset for this one? In a changing world, the credentials and capabilities of people in crucial positions must be constantly monitored and developed. Capability development at an operational level is often easier to identify. Our best clients also recognize that developing change readiness and leadership competence is key to implementing the action roadmap in a disciplined manner.

Driver: Process & Technology

A brilliant strategy, blockbuster product, or breakthrough technology can put you on the competitive map, but only solid execution can keep you there. You have to be able to deliver on your intent.

In order to maintain a high customer satisfaction rate and abide by contractual agreements, organizations need to create well-defined internal operating processes and procedures.

The challenge for organizations can be not just defining a best practice operational process that is linked to the new strategy, but assessing its level of effectiveness.

Ultimately, leaders should consider regularly performing a formal review of their operations and underpinning processes.

Technology also plays a crucial role. Technologies are already critical to strategy execution in many organizations, but as the global marketplace becomes more complex, they will only become more sophisticated. It almost goes without saying that information technology will give leaders more just-in-time information about how the company is faring, allowing them to continuously review plans, make course corrections, and quickly establish other complementary strategies as new opportunities emerge. The conventional once-a-year strategic planning process is likely to become much less common. Execution is also likely to be aided by refinements in technologies such as mobile computing, cloud-based data lakes, robotics, artificial intelligence, and an array of other efficiency-enhancing innovations. New technologies will also ramp up the speed of change and result in a more turbulent, hard-to-predict business environment. This will make it more difficult for some organizations to execute well while allowing others to gain definite strategic advantages via nimble strategy development and execution.

Sustain Momentum
If the finish line is in sight, can we afford to shift our focus onto the next race? Definitely not. In most cases,

getting to this stage has taken enormous effort, focus, and drive, and you should have reached a tipping point of success. As a leader, your role is to deliver on a number of tasks but to walk away just as the organization is benefiting from the momentum created through your execution to date would be suicidal at worst, ignorant at best.

Driver: Energy & Visibility
One driver where leaders consistently fail is in their inability to keep themselves or their teams enthused and energized over the entire length of the project. They often will initiate big launches and then take their eye off the ball. Your team needs to be continually reminded of the benefits of delivering their part of the plan—and just how much has already been achieved. It's not a question of making gung-ho motivational videos, but keeping key figures informed and rewarded in a way that is relevant to them.

How often is the leader seen by the workforce? Not just at the launch, but at every level of the follow-through? How is he or she identified with driving the strategy forward? How frequently will the leader have those really hard conversations with key policy-implementers to enforce that the desired policy changes are actually happening? Even if some are not naturally charismatic, leaders need to be seen, be vocal, be confident, and be novel in the way they project their commitment and their determination to see their vision acted upon.

Driver: Accountability

A key part of leadership is the ability to empower staff while creating a culture of positive accountability. Setting a clear model in the beginning makes it much easier for staff to see how and where they are succeeding or failing. People need to know what rewards they will get for delivery and what problems they will face for non-delivery. Imagine your organization as one where people are clear on the realistic strategy, believe that they can win, have personally chosen to go on the journey, and understand their priorities. Imagine also your people have been developed specifically to have the skills they need to deliver on their targets.

In our experience, if the leader has addressed each of these elements in turn, the task of embedding a culture of accountability is much easier.

Driver: Continuous Improvement

VTR is a loop, so continuous reflection and improvement is essential. An organization's capabilities and the drivers of strategy execution must be continually refreshed and renewed to remain aligned with changing customer expectations, altered competitive conditions, and new strategic initiatives.

By now, our clients are enjoying increased profitability from revenue stimulation and/or they have significant savings related to process and technology efficiencies and high levels of team engagement. Now is the time to invest in end-to-end revenue generation and sales solutions that include the best technology, people and practices to help the organization acquire new customers, retain them longer and grow their value.

How will you turn your Vision Into Results?
Successful leaders love being leaders – not for the sake of power but for the meaningful and purposeful impact they can create. When you have reached a senior level of leadership, success is about your ability to demonstrate applied leadership.

In the end, successful leaders are able to sustain their high levels of achievement because the 12 drivers of Vision to Results ultimately allows them to increase the value of their organization and its people; while at the same time minimizing the operating risk profile. They serve as the enablers of talent, culture and results.

Whether your vision involves revenue growth, effectiveness gains or the execution of strategic initiatives, we look forward to hearing your VTR stories and how you inspired exceptional performance and achieved extraordinary results.

About the authors

Glenn Price

Glenn Price is a strategy and leadership consultant with over 15 years' experience in leadership, sales management, strategy execution and change. Glenn has worked as a consultant in the Financial Services, Telecommunication and Technology sector – specializing in large global brands and has held a number of senior roles in Europe and the Middle East. He has a background in International Marketing and Law and has completed leadership programs at Harvard Business School. He has lectured in Behavioral Change Management for London Business School and the American University in Dubai.

Terry Reynolds

Terry Reynolds advises board members and executive teams in the financial services, energy and resources, public sector, and consumer business sectors. He maintains a portfolio of senior clients that he coaches 1:1 and has held a number of senior roles in Europe, the Middle East, Australasia. With postgraduate qualifications in Business Management, and experience as Director of Human Resources, development planning and program design, Terry has lectured at Murdoch University, Australia and the American University in Dubai. Terry is also highly experienced and licensed in a variety of diagnostic and profiling tools.

Scan this QR Code to visit the
Vision to Results website:

Download the free VTR
leadership coaching app.

Lightning Source UK Ltd.
Milton Keynes UK
UKOW06f0954161115

262818UK00001B/1/P